WHO IS MY NEIGHBOR?

Biblical Ministry in Our World of Diversity

Dr. Bill Thomas

Who Is My Neighbor?
Biblical Ministry in Our World of Diversity
Copyright © 2025 Bill Thomas

Published by College Press Publishing

Cover Design: Annie Halverson
Editing / formatting: Doug Reed

Unless otherwise indicated, all Scripture quotations are from the NIV® Bible (The Holy Bible, New International Version®), © 1973, 1978, 1984, 2011 by Biblica, Inc.™ Used by permission of Zondervan. All rights reserved worldwide. www.zondervan.com. The "NIV" and "New International Version" are trademarks registered in the United States patent and trademark Office by Biblica, Inc.™

ISBN 978-0-89900-183-8 (Paperback)
ISBN 978-0-89900-184-5 (E-book)

Endorsements

In a world that seems bent on division and hatred, it's important to hear what Bill Thomas says in, *Who is My Neighbor?* He reminds us of a critical truth—that we are one race, the human race. And as we seek to minister to our neighbors, we must remember that effective ministry only reaches across lines of difference when it is coated in unconditional love. As Thomas says, the church has a "wonderful opportunity to demonstrate the love, grace, compassion, and understanding that Jesus offers." This is a great book, not only for students, but for anyone wanting to serve Christ well.

T. Scott Womble, author of *The Pickoff*,
former VP of Academics at St. Louis Christian College

Who Is My Neighbor? addresses one of the most pressing and relevant questions facing the church: How do we minister faithfully and biblically across the deep divides in our society?

With theological depth, pastoral sensitivity, and practical clarity, Dr. Thomas builds a compelling case for multi-ethnic, gospel-centered ministry rooted in the unchanging truths of Scripture. Each chapter skillfully addresses foundational principles like authenticity, transformation, sustainability, and contemporary issues such as same-sex attraction, biblical justice, and ministry within broken families.

Who Is My Neighbor? calls the Church to reclaim its mission of disciple-making among all people through the lens of Christ's love and truth. I recommend this book to pastors, ministry leaders, and all believers seeking to engage our complex culture with conviction, compassion, and biblical clarity.

Dr. Ralph Baeza
Assistant Professor
Liberty University School of Divinity

Who is My Neighbor?

Dr. Bill Thomas reminds all of us in pastoral ministry and those in preparation for pastoral ministry that not everyone is like us! We all too often make our ministries in our own image. This book is a call to recognize the diversity and differences in people and communities that are often portrayed as obstacles to overcome, whereas Dr. Thomas reminds us that for the Church they are opportunities for grace and growth. Highly recommend anyone who is going into ministry or in ministry to read this book and reflect on opportunities our ministry contexts provides us.

James Riley Estep, Jr., D.Min., Ph.D.

Bill Thomas has addressed cultural and social issues that should grip readers' attention and provide practical application. His compelling biblical approach argues that all human beings are created in the image of God and are worthy of honor and respect regardless of their race or nationality. This book is grounded in sacred Scripture with research analysis that will make readers develop a biblical perspective on serving different communities and diverse groups with the message of the gospel.

Dr. Veerasammy Carpen, Author of *Sermon on the Mount*

Who is My Neighbor offers both a timely and biblically grounded approach to some of the most pressing issues facing the church and Christian higher education today. Thomas skillfully addresses the challenges of ministering across differences, rooting his arguments in Scripture, and drawing from various fields of study, while offering practical insights for real-world ministry. As someone passionate about equipping students for meaningful kingdom work, I found this book essential reading. It will inspire, challenge, and encourage anyone preparing for multicultural ministry to the next generation.

Page Brooks, Ph.D.
Missional Lead at Missio Mosaic: A Missional Society,
Prof. Theology & Culture, Mosaic Institute of Kairos University,
author of *Mergers and More: A Guide for Churches Who Don't Want to Die.*

Foreword

It took us a few minutes, but we eventually put the pieces together. Four of us from church stood in the living room of a mom, her pregnant daughter, and son-in-law. Yesterday they were homeless, but today they were in a safe, cool apartment on a hot, Tulsan day.

They were different than us, in more ways than we could count. I can't grasp what their life has been like. Homeless. Overheated. Pregnant. Scared. When I said we knew people often experienced loneliness when they moved to a new neighborhood, they nodded their heads. They were already wondering how to build new community.

Interactions like these remind me of the gravity of our obligation to love our neighbors. If we don't do it, everyone suffers: they suffer without the needed care and community we could provide, and we suffer without the ways they can draw us closer to the heartbeat of God, not to mention the dangerous, constant tug of apathy and selfishness that threatens us all.

All of this leads me to the million-dollar question: How in the world do we build God-honoring relationships with our neighbors who have different backgrounds, cultures, perspectives, values, or political preferences?

I'm so thankful that Bill Thomas goes there! Addressing the issues he tackles can feel like walking on the thinnest ice above the deepest waters. However, our families, churches, and communities need you to be formed by God, so we must walk on the ice.

Thank you for reading this work. Thank you for the courage, compassion, and commitment to loving God and loving our neighbors. Don't be discouraged by the challenging implications of this book. It's beautiful to learn and grow together. We'll all be better for it.

Brian Jennings
author of *Dancing in No Man's Land: Moving With Peace And Truth In A Hostile World*

Acknowledgements

I am grateful for the assistance of many people who contributed to this project.

I am thankful for Dr. Ralph Baeza, who was my mentor throughout the Dmin process and challenged me, almost from day one, to write this book.

I am also thankful to Brian Jennings who read an early draft, provided insights, and agreed to write the Foreword. I appreciate the willingness of all those who provided an endorsement for this book.

Special thanks go to Patricia Hicks, Crystal Applegarth, Cindy Bingamon, and Ericka Knoll who read and edited along the way to ensure a quality manuscript. I also appreciate the encouragement of the faculty, staff, and friends at Central Christian College of the Bible.

I also want to thank Karl Halverson and the team at College Press Publishing for their belief in the value of this book and their hard work bringing it to life.

As always, I am thankful for the support of my family.

Most of all, I am thankful for Jesus Christ. To him be glory forever and ever. Amen.

Contents

Endorsements	3
Foreword	5
Acknowledgements	7
Introduction	13

The Big Picture

Chapter 1

God's View of the City	19
The New Testament View of the City	23
The Ministry of Jesus and the City	26
Summing Up	30

Chapter 2

The Issue of Race	31
What is Different?	36
What Impact Does Race Have as a Social Construct?	37
Why Does the Discussion of Race and Ethnicity Matter?	40

Methodology

Chapter 3

Authenticity	45
What Does Authentic Ministry Look Like?	45
Benefits of Authentic Ministry	46
It's Not Your Way or the Highway	46
It Doesn't All Begin With You	49
No One's Perfect	53

Chapter 4

Caring	57
What is Poverty?	58
Where I've Seen Poverty	58
Is There A Better Way?	60
Process to Combat Poverty	63
Summing Up	64

Chapter 5
Transformation	67
Reconciliation with God	67
Concerns About Understanding Reconciliation	69
Reconciliation with Others	70
What Approach Will Work?	72
Walking With Jesus, Led by the Holy Spirit	72
Commitment to Discipleship	76

Chapter 6
Sustainability	79
What is Sustainability?	79
Why Do Some Ministries Not Make It?	80
Practical Strategies to Facilitate Sustainability	83
Sustainability Involves Recruiting and Training Leaders Well	85
Summing Up	87

Foundational Principles

Chapter 7
Theological Foundation	91
Summing Up	100

Chapter 8
Theoretical Foundations	101
Summing Up	109

Tough Issues

Chapter 9
Ministry to those of Same Sex Attraction	113
Be Aware of Spiritual Needs	114
Keep the Doors Open	114
Understand the Different Views About Same-Sex Attraction	116
Difficulty in Ministering to Those of Same-Sex Attraction	118
A Different Response to Same-Sex Attraction	119
What About the "T" of LGBT?	120
Summing Up	121

Chapter 10

    Biblical Justice   123
    What is Biblical Justice?   125
    Different Worldviews   129
    Summing Up   132

Chapter 11
    Nobody's Home   135
    Commitment to the Family   135
    Be Aware of the Challenges of Single Parents   136
    What Does Ministry to this Group Look Like?   138
    Ministry to Parents   138
    Ministry to Children   140
    Summing Up   143

Chapter 12
    Why It Matters   145
    What Does It Impact?   146
    The Restoration Movement Overview   150
    Final Picture   152

Bibliography   155
Endnotes   167

Introduction

Luke shares the story of when an expert in the law stood up to test Jesus. He wanted to know what he needed to do to inherit eternal life. Jesus asked him about what was written in the law. The law expert told him, "Love the Lord your God with all your heart and with all your soul and with all your strength and with all your mind" and "Love your neighbor as yourself." Jesus affirmed that answer and told him to do it. The expert then wanted to justify himself and his question, so he followed up with another question. He asked, "Who is my neighbor?" (Luke 10:25-29).

That question prompted one of Jesus' most popular parables. It is also a question that resonates today. Who is the Christian supposed to love? Who is the Christian supposed to serve? To whom is the Christian supposed to minister? For many, it comes down to *who is my neighbor?*

Americans live in a divided country. There are red and blue states, and the animosity between them is palpable. Recent elections have shown the country to be divided. Politics has devolved into attacking opponents, smearing their character, and belittling them in any way possible. There is little agreement on facts as news organizations slant coverage to fit the worldview of their audiences. Families argue over the issues of same-sex marriage and transgender rights. Racial tension still pulls hard at the fabric of our culture. Calls for justice echo throughout state houses across the land. Division has become the default setting for our country in many ways.

Culture is not the only area in which there are stark lines of disagreement. The church in the United States is also under pressure. There is a growing chasm between churches who hold to the authority of the Bible and those who have changed, accepting a more "progressive" approach. "Diversity, Equity and Inclusion" programs have been curtailed in some areas and have become a rallying call for others. Discussions about justice, equality, and unity energize people in both the church pew and on the Christian college campus, leading to a variety of opinions and ideas. There is no shortage of political approaches, but is there a better way? The church can and must offer biblical answers to provide clarity in the middle of chaos. How does the church do that? How can the church determine what issues are crucial, and which are matters of opinion? How can the church fulfill her mission in these divided times?

Despite the growing divide between people, the task of the church remains the same. Jesus said, "Therefore go and make disciples of all nations, baptizing them in the name of the Father and of the Son and of the Holy Spirit, and teaching them to obey everything I have commanded you. And surely, I am with you always, to the very end of the age" (Matt 28:19-20). The nature of God's kingdom is seen in this passage. God's desire is for people "of all nations" *(panta ta ethne)* to have a relationship with Him. D.A. Carson writes, "The aim of Jesus' disciples is to make disciples of all men everywhere, without distinction."[1] From the beginning, God has intended for the message of salvation to reach all people. Revelation 5:9-10 describes the song of the twenty-four elders. In that song, they proclaim, "with your blood you purchased for God persons from every tribe and language and people and nation." Gordon Fee writes of this passage, "John is affirming one of the frequent themes in the eschatological outlook of the Prophets—as well as the major passion in the ministry of Paul—that God chose Israel so that through them he might bless the whole world."[2] The point is clear: The church of Jesus Christ is to reflect the multi-ethnic nature of humanity.

Mark DeYmaz and Harry Li write, "The multi-ethnic church, like a good cup of coffee, produces an aroma that is refreshingly attractive—especially to those without Christ in an increasingly diverse and cynical society."[3] In the book of Revelation, the apostle John describes a multi-ethnic scene in heaven. He writes, "After this I looked, and there before me was a great multitude that no one could count, from every nation, tribe, people, and language, standing before the throne and before the Lamb. They were wearing white robes and were holding palm branches in their hands" (Rev 7:9). The multi-ethnic church demonstrates the nature of the Kingdom of God. It is God's desire that people of all languages, tribes, and nations worship Him.

DeYmaz writes, "The breaking down of ethnic, social, and cultural barriers is one of the strongest themes in Christ's ministry, and I believe Christ's Church should reflect both his character and his passion for all people."[4] Christ's character and His nature are reflected in the multitudes of different people who are citizens of his kingdom. The Bible is clear: The kingdom of God is comprised of people from *all* ethnicities and backgrounds. *They* are the answer to the question, "Who is my neighbor?" Ministry must reach across lines of difference if it is to be successful in the twenty-first century.

The Challenge for Christian Colleges and the Local Church

Christian colleges and the local church face challenges in fulfilling God's desire for all people to be a part of his kingdom. Christian colleges need to recommit to their mission of teaching and preparing men and women for a life of kingdom work in which they serve everyone. The local church has to embrace that which is different, which means asking hard questions about what has been comfortable and normal, about how things have always been done.

In the beginning, biblical higher education aimed to prepare and equip men and women for meaningful kingdom work. In the colonial period of the United States, most institutions of higher education were in the business of educating future ministers. Harvard and Yale, among others, were established under the goal of knowing Jesus Christ.[5] The biblical imperative to reach lost people was clear. When he ascended, Jesus told his disciples that they would be his witnesses "in Jerusalem, and in all Judea and Samaria, and to the ends of the earth" (Acts 1:8). Colleges and universities, from the outset, attempted to partner with churches to fulfill Jesus' mandate.

Beginning in the late nineteenth century, however, a change occurred in the nature and curriculum of many colleges. Secularism began to creep into established schools.[6] Denominations began to define issues differently. As the tide of theological liberalism washed over some schools, an opposition movement grew. In response to an increase of liberalism in colleges and universities in the late nineteenth century, many church groups, including the Restoration Movement (Christian Churches/Churches of Christ) of which I am a part, started their own Bible colleges. Johnson Bible College was one of the first of these and started as *The School of the Evangelists*, opening in 1893. More Bible colleges opened throughout the United States in the following four decades. The central core for these Restoration Movement schools was an emphasis on "biblical teaching."[7] These Bible colleges exist to teach and train students for ministry, both in the United States and in foreign mission fields.

It is crucial that Bible colleges remain faithful to that purpose. However, there is an area that has been historically neglected by the Restoration Movement Bible colleges, and others. Teaching students to minister effectively and confidently across the lines of racial, economic, and cultural differences, has not been prominent in many schools. The development of specific classes to prepare students for this kind of ministry would enable them to continue to reach lost people for Jesus Christ and add a biblical response to the discussion of these critical issues. The reality is, there are just not a lot of classes like that.

The church also has a role to play in helping people minister across lines of difference. The church of Jesus Christ can have incredible impact. Jesus told Simon Peter after his declaration that Jesus was the Messiah, "And I tell you that you are Peter, and on this rock I will build my church, and the gates of Hades will not overcome it" (Matt. 16:18). If there is any organization in today's culture that can bring diverse groups of people together, it is the church. While there are no specific numbers with respect to how diverse a congregation ought to be, the body of Christ in any given place ought to be reflective of the people in that place. Local church bodies must ask themselves if they are open to reaching all the people that God has placed around them and to tear down any walls.

It is important for the body of Christ to examine this issue. Can ministry students be taught to minister across lines of differences more effectively? Teaching ministry students to cross lines of racial, cultural, and socio-economic differences will move the church closer to Jesus' prayer "that all of them be one" (John 17:21). When ministers and church leaders are challenged and motivated to pursue that, they can lead others in that same walk. I pray this book will inspire leaders to take one more step in that journey.

The Big Picture

Chapter 1

God's View of the City

The city is crucial in God's plan for humanity and ministering across lines of difference must address how to interact with the city. In the twenty-first century, the word "city" evokes images of millions of people, tall buildings, and a sense of hurry. Sometimes the word "city" produces pictures of poverty and problems. Timothy Keller challenges the contemporary understanding of what a city is when writing, "We must be careful, however, not to impose our current cultural understanding of city onto the biblical term. The most common Hebrew word for city, *'ir*, meant any human settlement surrounded by some fortification or wall." He further asserts that according to the Bible, total population is not what defined a city, but population density.[8] Understanding what constitutes a city is important in determining how to best minister to a city.

Effective ministry to the city is a biblical imperative. Luke notes Jesus' words as he ascended into heaven, "But you will receive power when the Holy Spirit comes on you and you will be my witnesses in Jerusalem, and in all Judea and Samaria and to the ends of the earth" (Acts 1:8). The place where the disciples were first challenged to share the good news was in the city of Jerusalem. Evangelism began in the city. What was true from the beginning of Christianity is also true now. Keller asserts, "Every city in the world needs Jesus Christ. But our cities do not merely need a few more churches and ministries here and there; they need gospel city movements that lead to city-wide tipping points."[9] God loves people, and he sent Jesus to die for them (John 3:16) and to change their lives. From the start, the city has been a part of God's plan because cities are a wide range of diverse people and not buildings.

In the Bible, the city of God is clearly noted. John records a multitude in heaven that reflects the diverse nature of the city. "After this I looked, and there before me was a great multitude that no one could count, from every nation, tribe, people, and language, standing before the throne and before the Lamb. They were wearing white robes and were holding palm branches in their hands. And they cried out in a loud voice: 'Salvation belongs to our God, who sits on the throne, and to the Lamb'" (Rev 7:9-10). From the early chapters of Genesis to the resounding conclusion of the Revelation, it is clear God wants to dwell with his people in his city. T. Desmond Alexander writes, "With remarkable conciseness the opening chapters of Genesis introduce a story that looks forward to the creation of an exceptional city where God and humanity will live in harmony."[10] Early passages of Genesis reveal that the city God planned was far from being realized. From Cain building a city and naming it after his son Enoch, to the founding of Babel/Babylon, "the human ambition to construct alternative, godless cities"[11] was evident. However, godless cities were not what God intended. Envisioning the glorious city God desired, the Psalmist wrote, "He has founded his city on the holy mountain. The Lord loves the gates of Zion more than all the other dwellings of Jacob. Glorious things are said of you, city of God" (Psalms 87:1-3). Alexander notes, "Here, the city of God is clearly linked to a holy Mount Zion."[12] He also describes the thrust of the Old Testament books Exodus and Leviticus: "In essence, Exodus and Leviticus record how God orientates the Israelites toward holy living, an essential requirement for all citizens of the city of God."[13] The city God intends is powerfully described by John in Revelation: "I saw the Holy City, the new Jerusalem, coming down out of heaven from God, prepared as a bride beautifully dressed for her husband. And I heard a loud voice from the throne saying, 'Look! God's dwelling place is now among the people, and he will dwell with them. They will be his people, and God himself will be with them and be their God'" (Rev. 21:2-3). Ministry to the diverse groups of the city is important, and it makes a difference. Many urban churches can be revitalized and experience new life, regardless of how close they are to dying. The time has never been better for such a transformation to happen.[14] The Bible provides three truths that illuminate God's relationship with the city.

The Big Picture   Chapter 1

God's Purpose for the City

Jesus, before he ascended, told the disciples that the Holy Spirit would empower them to be his witnesses, beginning in Jerusalem (Acts 1:8). The city of Jerusalem was the launching point for the message of Jesus. The message of Jesus would spread from there to cities around the world. It is crucial to understand that cities are not an amalgamation of buildings, homes, and streets. Cities, at the core, are people.

The dispersion of Christians from Jerusalem enabled the message of Jesus to spread to the cities of the world. Christians fled Jerusalem and took the gospel with them. There is another dispersion happening today. Residents of cities in communist countries are moving out of those cities and into cities where the Christian faith is vibrant. Ministries in those cities have a growing opportunity to do meaningful kingdom work. Kiêu Công Thuân writes, "The Vietnamese diaspora is part of the plan of God to scatter them in Christian countries so that they can hear and respond to the Gospel. They are successful economically and educationally, but not missionally. Thus, reaching and training this community is practically and essentially important."[15]

The city was significant in the first century and even more so in the twenty-first century. Because of the sheer number of people in the city, God intends for evangelism and ministry to thrive and grow there. The message then can spread, sometimes from the city to the areas surrounding it, and at other times to those who migrate to that city from other places. In both circumstances, God continues to have plans for the city.

Sin Hinders God's Plan for the City

God's plan for the city is evident, but sin tarnished what God planned for good. Alexander asserts that city building, from the beginning, has been in the DNA of human beings. It is what God intended for humans to do. However, he observes that man's selfishness and sin corrupted God's intent. It is noteworthy that Cain named the city he built after his son, Enoch. By doing so he glorified his

21

son rather than the one who gifted him to be a builder.[16] Human beings, from the start, sought to build to glorify themselves. A glance through the Old Testament reveals humanity's misguided attempt to steal the glory that should belong to God. Cain's attempt to build a city to honor his own son was only the beginning. In Genesis 11, after the flood, the people decided to build a city and a tower. Their motivation for building was also revealed in Genesis 11:4: "Then they said, "Come, let us build ourselves a city, with a tower that reaches to the heavens, so that we may make a name for ourselves; otherwise, we will be scattered over the face of the whole earth." Allen P. Ross writes of this passage, "The purpose of their building venture was fame. They wished to find security by arrogantly making a name — a desire that is satirized in verse nine." The results were not what the builders hoped. "Their greatest fear came on them. The place of unity became the place of dispersion."[17] The prideful city doomed to dispersion was Babel. Alexander summarizes this scene succinctly, "Babel epitomizes the antithesis of what God desires."[18]

Babylon, from a human perspective, was a great, powerful city. In Babylon, there was a seven-storied tower with a temple top that was known as *E-temen-ank*, dedicated to their god Marduk, that became one of the wonders of the world.[19] The Lord God judged the arrogance, godlessness, and evil of Babylon. "You said, 'I am forever—the eternal queen!' But you did not consider these things or reflect on what might happen" (Isa 47:7). Jeremiah also foretold God's judgment against the arrogance of Babylon. "See, I will stir up the spirit of a destroyer against Babylon and the people of Leb Kamai. I will send foreigners to Babylon to winnow her and to devastate her land; they will oppose her on every side in the day of her disaster" (Jer 51:1-2). The great city of humanity, built on pride, founded on sin and rebellion, will ultimately fall (Rev 18:2).

Sin corrupted God's plan for a city in which he could dwell with his people. Unhappiness and injustice displace peace and disrupt order. God created and intended everything to be orderly and just. Human sin disrupted the order God intended for his people. Because of sin, the city is not as God intends it to be, but God has not given up on the city. He has a plan for a glorious city in which he will dwell with his people forever.

The Big Picture   Chapter 1

God's Plan for a Glorious City

Throughout Genesis and Exodus, the narrative focuses on the growth, enslavement, and deliverance of God's people. They are on a quest for the Promised Land. One of the results of that will be the establishment of Jerusalem. Alexander writes, "Jerusalem is important as the location of God's earthly residence, which is reflected in the annual religious pilgrimages undertaken by the Israelites."[20] Psalm 48:1-2 reflects the glory of Jerusalem as God's earthly city: "Great is the Lord, and most worthy of praise, in the city of our God, his holy mountain. Beautiful in its loftiness, the joy of the whole earth, like the heights of Zaphon is Mount Zion, the city of the Great King." The significance of Jerusalem is evident in these words of the Lord: "Since the day I brought my people out of Egypt, I have not chosen a city in any tribe of Israel to have a temple built so that my Name might be there, nor have I chosen anyone to be ruler over my people Israel. But now I have chosen Jerusalem for my Name to be there, and I have chosen David to rule my people Israel" (2 Chr 6:5-6).

As glorious as the earthly city of Jerusalem was in God's sight, it does not compare to the glory of the eternal city of God, New Jerusalem. That city is prophetically seen in the Old Testament. Alexander writes of the Israelites, "that they are responsible for establishing the temple-city of Jerusalem. While this development is significant, it is only a part of God's plan for the completion of his creation blueprint."[21] The completion is found in the eternal city of God. Writing of that glorious city, Isaiah noted, "The moon will be dismayed, the sun ashamed; for the Lord Almighty will reign on Mount Zion and in Jerusalem, and before its elders—with great glory" (Isa 24:23). Isaiah also spoke prophetically of New Jerusalem: "See, I will create new heavens and a new earth. The former things will not be remembered, nor will they come to mind. But be glad and rejoice forever in what I will create, for I will create Jerusalem to be a delight and its people a joy" (Isa 65:17-18).

The New Testament View of the City

Not only does the Old Testament address God's desire for a city in which he can dwell with his people, the New Testament also addresses the importance of the cities in which Jesus and the apostles ministered. Raymond J. Bakke writes, "Acts 2 reports the first hours of the church's existence as being both international and multilingual. For Luke— the urbane, European, Gentile historian— the story of the early church was meant to document how this Jewish movement from the distant frontier city of Jerusalem could become the faith comprehensive and inclusive enough for the Roman Empire and its leadership."[22] Writing in the context of the high priest and the city of Jerusalem, the writer of Hebrews notes, "For here we do not have an enduring city, but we are looking for the city that is to come" (Heb. 13:14). From the beginning of the church, God's desire was to dwell with people. The church was to reach cities. The goal was, as was foreseen in the Old Testament, an eternal city of God. The New Testament addresses the city with respect to two different components.

Reconciliation

The city of God in the New Testament is concerned about reconciliation. Bakke explains the parameters of justice and reconciliation are set by noting the nature and purpose of God's kingdom: "The reign of God has begun, but it is also yet to come in its fullness. This means the salvation message goes beyond the merely personal to address our whole society, its structures, and its systems."[23] Harry Louis Williams writes, "Jesus proclaimed his messiahship by stating that God had anointed him to help the most marginalized people in society, that God had anointed him to massage salve into the wounds of those who were bruised."[24] Jesus' ministry and proclamation of the kingdom (city of God) dealt with justice and reconciliation. Jesus rebuked the religious leaders of his day when he chided, "Woe to you, teachers of the law and Pharisees, you hypocrites! You give a tenth of your spices—mint, dill, and cumin. But you have neglected the more important matters of the law—justice, mercy, and faithfulness. You should have practiced the latter, without neglecting the former" (Matt 23:23).

Jesus proclaimed a message of justice or the righting of wrongs, but it has a much broader context than how justice is often understood. The thrust of justice, as taught by Jesus, was to bring reconciliation. Paul wrote, "And he has committed to us the message of reconciliation. We are therefore Christ's ambassadors, as though God were making his appeal through us. We implore you on Christ's behalf: Be reconciled to God" (2 Cor. 5:19-20). Susan Baker notes, "God is a God of justice, mercy, and reconciliation. Taking this message seriously is at the heart of ministry in a global world."[25] Romans 12–15 is a passage that describes, in a practical way, how citizens of God's city are to live. It is summarized well, "Do not be overcome by evil, but overcome evil with good" (Romans 12:21). The New Testament strongly declares that justice, with the aim toward reconciliation, is a component of the city of God.

Barrier Breaking

The city of God, as described by the New Testament, is also about breaking barriers. This important aspect is crucial and can be seen in how the church impacted New Testament cities. The first of the barriers that fall as the church emerges in the book of Acts, is the language barrier. Bakke observes, "We should not be surprised that the 120 believers in the upper room knew all the languages spoken at Pentecost; they came from all those places. For the first time, under the influence of the Holy Spirit, all those languages were used in worship in Jerusalem. From then on, the church's worship would be multilingual in the heart of a city where one language was official, but many others were spoken by the people."[26] The early church was born in a multilingual city. Luke notes the significance of this: "Now there were staying in Jerusalem God-fearing Jews from every nation under heaven. When they heard this sound, a crowd came together in bewilderment, because each one heard their own language being spoken" (Acts 2:5-6). Craig Keener notes a parallel to Babel, the prideful city of humanity in the Old Testament. He writes of this passage, "God scattered nations at Babel for trying to deify themselves (Gen 11:4), paralleling Adam's revolt and his expulsion from the garden (3:5, 22-23). By contrast, the disciples at Pentecost were waiting in obedience to a divine command (Acts 1:4-5); instead of trying to reach heaven, they were waiting for their Lord, who had ascended to heaven (1:9-11), to send them the Spirit."[27]

Other cultural barriers were broken down by the church in connection with the coming city of God. These include ethnocentric and gender ones. Acts 6 is the place in the life of the church, where these barriers are first addressed. There is a problem in the church about the distribution of food, specifically to the Greek widows. Seven men were appointed to handle this ministry. The problem began with an ethnic group being ignored. The solution not only broke down that wall but also challenged gender stereotypes. Bakke writes, "It is highly instructive to notice that the 'great' Stephen and Philip began their apostolic careers doing what people today sometimes call 'women's work.' Luke is documenting the cultural shifts and bridges that must be crossed if our churches are to detribalize and include the whole city."[28] Further ethnocentric boundaries are pushed in Luke's gospel. His account of the Good Samaritan in Luke 10 and the Samaritan leper who returned to give thanks in Luke 11, resonate with the message, "The whole gospel is for the whole world."[29] There will be no racial, gender, or ethnic separations in the city of God. It will be for all people.

The church in Antioch represents how the city of God is for the whole world. Bakke writes of the nature of Antioch: "A great center of trade, commerce and scholarship, Antioch was the third largest city in the empire, after Rome and Alexandria, with between 500,000 and 800,000 residents."[30] He continues, "Apparently, in Antioch, people of different ethnic backgrounds began to cross the interior walls of the city to hear the gospel and join the church."[31] Jeff Iorg writes, "Antioch is an ancient model for the future church. This church, composed of transformed people, transformed its community, the Mediterranean region, and the world as we know it."[32] Antioch, the place where the disciples were first called Christians, resounds with all the distinctions that will encompass the city of God. The New Testament vividly portrays the dynamic nature of the gospel in the cities of that time. The impact the gospel had on those cities foreshadows the nature of the coming city of God.

The Ministry of Jesus and the City

William David Spencer writes, "For Jesus, two positive images are linked together: light and the city. His disciples are supposed to be a source of light for everyone else— as obvious and unashamed as a great metropolis, resplendent on the highest promontory, presiding over everything, influencing culture, setting the standard, establishing the trends, making itself the center, the reference point to which everyone else in the population turns for knowledge, for enlightenment, for healing."[33] Ministry to the city cannot be separated from Jesus' ministry. Jesus' heart and passion were for the city. His ministry to the city can be examined in three ways. Looking at these three ways results in the church's challenge.

A Connecting Point

Jesus' ministry was about connecting with people, meeting their needs, and ultimately their greatest need for a Savior. Paul writes, "He came and preached peace to you who were far away and peace to those who were near. For through him we both have access to the Father by one Spirit" (Ephesians 2:17-18). Jesus came to connect diverse people (Jews and Gentiles). He also came to connect these diverse groups to God. Spencer writes, "A city can be defined as a network of relationships. The reason for a city's existence, after all, is to connect. Everything in it is networked. In essence, the city is itself a container of connections."[34] God's desire is to interact with his people. His city in the old covenant was Jerusalem, but humanity was drawn to Babylon. His new covenant city is New Jerusalem. What exists on earth today, according to Spencer, are "cities of Enoch,"[35] Spencer notes the challenge of the church today as he writes: "We have to band together and act to take back our communities. The divinely appointed task of assisting God in reconciling the world, demands we adjust the values of our communities to those of God's New Jerusalem, rebuilding our own cities of Enoch on the blueprints of Christ."[36]

Williams cites the importance of connecting: "You have to be out in this world, out in these streets among the people on a consistent basis to develop the sort of empathy and compassion for people that stretch you to do all you can to make a difference."[37] This is at the heart of Jesus' ministry and teaching. Jesus taught, "Truly I tell you, whatever you did for one of the least of these brothers and sisters of mine, you did for me" (Matt. 25:40). Connecting was at the heart of Jesus' ministry and it must be at the heart of ministry across lines of racial, cultural, and socio-economic difference.

Passion for the Marginalized

Jesus cared for those on the margins of society, which can be observed in several New Testament examples. His encounter with the woman at the well in Samaria stands out. She was so surprised he spoke to her, she remarked, "You are a Jew, and I am a Samaritan woman. How can you ask me for a drink?" For Jews do not associate with Samaritans (John 4:9). We also see Jesus interacting on the margins in his encounter with the leper after the Sermon on the Mount. Jesus did the unthinkable in that culture. He "reached out and touched the man" that no one else would touch. He brought him healing, hope, and a new life (Matt. 8:1-4). Mark Harden writes, "When the church engages effectively in the redemptive work of God, the people and spaces in the city become communal spaces that reflect a church 'reaching for the New Jerusalem.'"[38] Donald McGavran observes the reason the church is to reach out to the marginalized and those in need. He writes, "The founding mission or church establishes schools, hospitals, agricultural centers, literacy classes, and many other institutions to serve and help the general public and specially the new brothers in Christ."[39]

Ministry to the marginalized goes beyond creating institutions to minister. That is a crucial mission, but not the only mission for the church with respect to the marginalized. Luke 4:17 notes what Jesus read in the synagogue: "The Spirit of the Lord is on me, because he has anointed me to proclaim good news to the poor. He has sent me to proclaim freedom for the prisoners and recovery of sight for the blind, to set the oppressed free, to proclaim the year of the Lord's favor." Susan Baker quotes S.D. Gaude: "If we are not on the side of both truth and justice, we are not on God's side."[40] Jesus, as the Messiah, brought freedom, healing, and restoration. The church, if she is to fulfill her calling, must respond appropriately to the needs of the marginalized population.

The Big Picture

The question of how to do this is a big one. This issue gets traction in the political realm, but racial issues, justice and breaking down barriers are larger than a political party, agenda, or solution. The driving force behind the church reaching for "New Jerusalem" is *reconciliation*. Baker writes, "God has come in Jesus to renew the world, to make what is broken whole."[41] The key is to exalt Jesus Christ. He is the one that makes wrong things right. He is the one who takes what is broken and makes it whole. Jesus stated, "And I, when I am lifted up from the earth, will draw all people to myself" (John 12:32).

Unity

One of most important components of Jesus' ministry and that of his church is to promote unity. He prayed, "My prayer is not for them alone. I pray also for those who will believe in me through their message, that all of them may be one, Father, just as you are in me, and I am in you. May they also be in us so that the world may believe that you have sent me (John 17:20-21). Lorraine Cleaves Anderson writes of one unique way that is growing in popularity: "One powerful, emerging paradigm, particularly visible in urban areas, is space-sharing within church buildings."[42] Doing so allows for a mixing of cultures and a shared sense, not only of space, but of purpose. Anderson continues, "To share our resources gladly and equitably, we will, by default, find ourselves practicing radical reciprocity with new friends and colleagues. We will discover a freedom indeed that nourishes not the kingdom of 'First Urban Church,' but the kingdom of God, citywide— the New Jerusalem."[43] Roger J. Gench explains it this way: "The church was called into being to embody and engage a ministry of reconciliation for the purpose of building redemptive, liberating, and covenantal relationships; but even in church we can become so task-oriented that we easily lose sight of our calling."[44] According to Gench, the church is to build relationships with all kinds of people, and he notes it is easy to lose sight of that calling. It was Jesus' desire and the church's mission that his followers be one.

Summing Up

There will come a day when the people of God will live together with him in the City of God and it will be wonderful and amazing. John's writing describes the City of God: "The city does not need the sun or the moon to shine on it, for the glory of God gives it light, and the Lamb is its lamp. The nations will walk by its light, and the kings of the earth will bring their splendor into it" (Rev 21:23-24). The glory of that city and the joy of that day are evident. Alexander notes that what Christians do today is in preparation for citizenship in God's great city: "For those who are united to Jesus Christ, eternal life begins here and now, as does citizenship of the city that will one day be created by God on a renewed earth."[45]

There is a unique calling for those who do urban ministry. Working with the cities of earth, demonstrating to them the love of Jesus Christ and the opportunity of eternal life in him, foreshadows the nature of God's City. Bakke wrote, "Pastoring in the city is an art that requires helping congregations define their identity and security in the church universal, while creating a climate for diverse worship and ministry styles that can bridge generations, classes and cultural backgrounds."[46] At the end of the parable of the persistent widow, Jesus asks a question that is still relevant for ministers and ministries today: "When the Son of Man comes, will he find faith on the earth?" (Luke 18:8b).

Chapter 2

The Issue of Race

Teaching to minister effectively across lines of racial, cultural, and socio-economic differences must begin with an honest look at the issue of race in the United States. Issues surrounding race continue to stir the emotions of Americans in the third decade of the twenty-first century. There are a few significant truths that have to be acknowledged regarding race and the American culture.

First, racism and prejudice are real. From the lynching of Emmet Till in 1955 to the murder of Ahmaud Arbery in 2020, with many incidents in between and after, the color of a person's skin has been a factor in how that person has been treated. It is ugly and must be called out for what it is, sin. The church has not been immune to the stain of racism and many Christian colleges and Bible colleges began in a time of racial strife and unrest.

Central Christian College of the Bible is a Restoration Movement college in Moberly, Missouri, which opened in 1957. In Moberly, the public library is named The Little Dixie Regional Library largely because the area around Moberly, since the late 1800s, has been known as "Little Dixie." Incidents of racial unrest, violence, and injustice are scattered throughout the town's history.

In November 1919, a white farmer in Moberly accused four African American men of beating and robbing him. Halley Richardson, Sanford Taylor, George Adams, and James Anderson, all twenty years old or younger, were arrested and jailed in Macon, Missouri. Late one night a mob of one hundred and fifty drove to Macon and demanded that Sheriff Jesse Stamper let them in to get the four men. Stamper gave in to the mob who took the four to a park on the west side of town. They tried to hang the four of them from one branch of a tree, but it broke. One of the four was shot as he tried to stand.

Who is My Neighbor?

The other three ran away only to be recaptured. This is one of many incidents that happened in the area known as "Little Dixie."[47]

In the fall of 1955, just two years before Central Christian College of the Bible opened, seven black public-school teachers at the Lincoln School, the black school in Moberly, were let go after the 1954 Supreme Court decision Brown v. Topeka Board of Education prohibited state-sanctioned segregation of public schools. The school district of Moberly, in compliance with the Supreme Court's decision, decided to close the Lincoln School. The teachers claimed the school district of Moberly denied them reemployment because of their race. They claimed the Moberly School District had a policy, at that time, not to hire black teachers for schools in which white children attended. The defendants denied that such a policy existed and that the black teachers were not hired because they were not as qualified as white teachers. The trial court found in favor of the school district. The United States Court of Appeals for the Eighth Circuit upheld the verdict in a June 17, 1959, opinion.[48] This ruling, while unquestioned in 1959, is viewed differently today. This was the climate in Moberly around the time of the founding of Central Christian College of the Bible.

Central's story is one of many. Culture and laws are not the same now as they were in the mid-1950's, and not every accusation of racism rings true. However, there is no denying the reality of racial prejudice. It is something that the church and Christian higher education must confront.

Second, discussions about race elicit a wide range of opinions and ideas. White supremacy is routinely discussed in news reports and on social media. There are those who believe white supremacy to be the greatest threat to our country. Ramon Gutierrez posits, "Fringe and mainstream manifestations of white supremacy work together as part of a social structure, enabling the continuation of racist violence and policymaking."[49] Others believe that while white supremacy is a vile teaching, its influence and outreach are overstated. A Marist poll in 2021 noted that nearly half, forty-eight percent, of Americans do not believe white supremacy to be the "most lethal threat to the homeland."[50] This issue continues to be debated from coffee shops to congressional hearing rooms. Another issue that has arisen in the American culture is the issue of potential reparations. This discussion is seen on social media platforms and discussed among the talking heads on cable news networks. For some, this is long, overdue justice. Charles Henry, noting judicial action, observes, "lawsuits charged that institutions that owned, used, or insured slaves violated domestic and international law by conspiring to deprive the slaves and their descendants of their property."[51] While none of these lawsuits has won in court, proponents of reparations continue to work. For others, however, this is another example of government overreach. A 2021 UMass Amherst poll indicates that about two thirds of Americans oppose providing reparations to those whose family members were slaves.[52] The issue of reparations is one that is not likely to disappear. Even something as simple as who is admitted into college can stir racial discussions. In the spring of 2023, the Supreme Court ruled that colleges and universities can no longer legally utilize race-based admissions policies. Some hailed this as a victory for meritocracy, while others viewed it as an attack on minority students. Discussions about race seem to be everywhere in every medium and there is no shortage of opinions regarding these issues. The church and the Bible college must engage in these discussions. If a biblical perspective is vital and correct, who will bring that perspective to the table if the church and those in Christian higher education do not?

The third observation is simple and direct. There is only one race, the human race. This observation seems contrary to the prevailing cultural opinion. Students fill out forms asking them to identify their race. The census bureau identifies five specific categories of race: Black or African American, White, American Indian/Alaskan Native, Asian, and Native Hawaiian or Pacific Islander. It is important to understand people are different. For example, medical doctors see it in how people respond to certain medicines. It does, then, seem ridiculous to assert that there is but one race. However, both science and the Bible make the argument that the differences between various people groups are insignificant and that humans have far more in common with each other than they recognize. Recognition of this fact is vital if ministry across lines of racial, cultural, and socio-economic differences is to be effective.

Who is My Neighbor?

What Does the Scientific Community Say About Race?

Children used to be taught the song "Jesus Loves the Little Children of the World." The song says, "Red, yellow, black and white, they are precious in his sight." While the message of the song is good, the science is not. Human beings are not "red, yellow, black and white." They are all varying shades of brown. Melanin is the skin's brown pigment. Darker skin is the presence of more melanin while lighter skin indicates the presence of less melanin. The difference in skin tone is due, in part, to the combination of genes that govern the amount of melanin in each person. There also may be some adaptation at work with respect to skin tone. Darker skin may have been the adaptation that prevailed near the equator where the strength of ultraviolet light was greater. Lighter skin may have become dominant in northern areas where exposure to ultraviolet light was less. It is important to note, despite the observable differences among people, human beings are far more alike than they are different.

Biologists and geneticists confirm that assertion. Human beings, at their DNA core, are virtually the same. Robin DiAngelo posits that "the differences we do see with our eyes, such as hair texture and eye color are superficial and emerged as adaptations to geography. There really is no race under the skin."[53] The National Human Genome Research Institute states, "All human beings are 99.9 percent identical in their genetic makeup."[54] Megan Gannon writes in the *Scientific American*, "Today, the mainstream belief among scientists is that race is a social construct without biological meaning."[55] The evidence from those in the scientific community indicates that race, as it is commonly defined, has no basis in biology. According to many in the scientific world, with respect to genetics, human beings are nearly the same.

Race is a social construct that has been applied to different people groups based on their similarities. The term "race" is often used to biologically distinguish groups of people who have different social or cultural backgrounds. There is no biological basis for the race determinations that are made in twenty-first century culture. The term "race" will likely continue to be used in conversation, however, those in ministry should recognize that it is not a legitimate difference. The scientific community seems unified with regard to the question of race. All people are of the human race.

Racist Roots in Darwinian Thought

Science has not always viewed race this way. Charles Darwin is a well-known name in the scientific community. He was an English biologist, naturalist, and geologist that made huge contributions to the discussion of evolutionary biology. Darwin, however, may have also contributed to the idea that there are more than one race of humans and that some races are superior to others. The full title of his most famous work is *On the Origin of Species by Means of Natural Selection, or the Preservation of Favored Races in the Struggle for Life.* Darwin theorized that simple life evolved into higher life forms through the forces of nature selecting the fittest. In his book *The Descent of Man,* Darwin asserted that some races were more evolved or developed than others. He labels them "civilized races" and "lower races." Darwin writes, "We will now look to the intellectual faculties alone. If in each grade of society, the members were divided into two equal bodies, the one including the intellectually superior and the other the inferior, there can be little doubt that the former would succeed best in all occupations."[56] Richard Weikart summarizes Darwin's thought: "T*he Descent of Man,* in other words, argues quite explicitly for 'the preservation of favored' human races in the struggle for life."[57] This teaching spread widely throughout Europe and the United States in the 1800's.

In the late 1800's Darwin's ideas were used to justify certain political, social, and economic views. Collectively, these thoughts morphed into what is now called "Social Darwinism." Social Darwinists apply Darwin's theory of natural selection regarding plants and animals to the study of individuals, people groups and cultures. Simply put, Social Darwinists believe that certain people become powerful in society because they are innately better. This idea is clearly repugnant to most people today and is definitely not a biblical view. Ken Ham writes, "In *The Descent of Man,* Darwin popularized the idea of different races of people — lower races, higher races, primitive races, advanced races." Ham asserts, "Darwinian evolution was (and still is) inherently a racist philosophy. It teaches that different groups or 'races' of people evolved at different times and rates. According to his theory, some groups are more like (and closer to) their ape-like ancestors than others."[58] It is difficult not to see racism in some of Darwin's views and writings, and especially in how others have used his works.

The Bible

In contrast to the Social Darwinists, the Bible demonstrates clearly that there is only one race of people, human. Genesis 1:27 records the creation of human beings: "So God created mankind in his own image, in the image of God he created them; male and female he created them." It is evident from this passage that God created Adam and Eve singularly in his image. There is no other biblical account that details a separate creation of another human race. Adam and Eve were the first of a single race the encompasses all of humanity. All human beings trace their roots to Adam and Eve. Paul, in his sermon to the Athenians, notes: "From one man he (God) made all the nations, that they should inhabit the whole earth; and he marked out their appointed times in history and the boundaries of their lands" (Acts 17:26). Paul's point is clear, God is the one who made the world and all that's in it. He gives people life, breath, and everything else. In fact, he made all people through one person so that people would seek him and perhaps reach out for him. The biblical record supports the same conclusion that science advances, there is only one race, human.

What is Different?

While there is only one human race, there are different nationalities and ethnicities. Biblically, ethnicity (*ethnos* in Greek or *goy* in Hebrew) refers to a tribe, nation, or people group. These often have different languages and live in different locations. Both the Bible and science agree with that assertion. From a biblical perspective, different nationalities exist as a result of the dispersion at Babel in Genesis 11. Genesis 11:1-2 notes, "Now the whole world had one language and a common speech. As people moved eastward, they found a plain in Shinar and settled there." Notice that the whole world had one language, a common speech, and they were unified. That unity, however, was not used for good. Then they said, "Come, let us build ourselves a city, with a tower that reaches to the heavens, so that we may make a name for ourselves; otherwise, we will be scattered over the face of the whole earth" (Gen 11:4). "The purpose of the city was so that its inhabitants would not be scattered over the face of the whole earth. Ironically, at the conclusion of the story, it is the Lord who scattered the builders from the city."[59] God longed for and still longs for his people to be unified. However, he refused to allow them to unify in an attempt to glorify themselves, so he scattered them. They spoke different languages and developed into different ethnicities.

Though people sinned, God's desire to unify the different people groups of the world has not changed. Timothy Keller notes, "At Babel, people of one speech could not understand one another, because they were trying to reach up to heaven in their own strength to make a name for themselves. At Pentecost, people of many speeches were all able to understand God's message. At Pentecost, God reversed the curse of Babel through the work of his Son."[60] On the Day of Pentecost, Jews from all over the world heard the gospel in their own language. The Day of Pentecost was the spiritual reversal of the sin of Babel. The possibility for the unity of different ethnicities and people groups is found only in the person and work of Jesus.

What Impact Does Race Have as a Social Construct?

While the evidence for there being only one race is indisputable, those who minister across lines of difference will inevitably have to wrestle with a culture that has emphasized racial differences. As noted by Loritts, "The church that plays offense when it comes to race is the kind of church that will never settle for diversity but will be committed to ethnic unity nurtured through a relentless commitment to having substantive relationships with the other."[61] What does "going on offense" look like?

Be Honest

Paul writes, "Therefore each of you must put off falsehood and speak truthfully to your neighbor, for we are all members of one body" (Eph 4:25). Solomon observes, "The Lord detests lying lips, but he delights in people who are trustworthy" (Prov 12:22). Both the Old and New Testament speak of honesty and integrity. God desires his people to be honest. Honesty is an important quality for the minister. Being honest with respect to ministry across lines of difference, especially concerning racial issues, is crucial if that ministry is to succeed.

Honesty, in this context, seeks to hear and acknowledge another person. It is not about being heard or sharing your story. It is about listening and understanding where the other person is. Honesty is also the courage to call out sin when it happens. For example, it is right to critique those of one's own tribe if they are wrong. Historically, how some in the Restoration Movement viewed slavery was not in line with the Bible. That is a statement of fact. Honesty requires that truthful assessments be made. Understanding that law enforcement does not always interact with minority groups the same as they do with others is an honest observation. It is also honest to acknowledge that not all encounters that members of minority groups have with police are racist or examples of brutality. These kinds of discussions are not easy, nor are they always comfortable. However, if we are to successfully minister across lines of difference, we must have a common commitment to the truth. Successful ministry across lines of difference demands honesty.

Be Loving

Paul writes, "And over all these virtues put on love, which binds them all together in perfect unity" (Col 3:14). Peter challenges his readers: "Above all, love each other deeply, because love covers over a multitude of sins" (1 Pet 4:8). In both of these texts, the word for love is from the root word, *agape*. Both writers are talking about unconditional love. Christians are called to love others unconditionally and it is this unconditional love that binds together compassion, kindness, humility, gentleness, and patience. Unconditional love is what can cover a multitude of sins and is a part of the Christian's DNA.

Unconditional love is a vital component of ministry across lines of difference, especially in the context of race. The definition of racism notes that "it is a belief that race is a fundamental determinant of human traits and capacities and that racial differences produce an inherent superiority of a particular race."[62] Racism and prejudice presuppose people to be superior or inferior based on external appearance and assign value or worth based on those external traits. Racism is the opposite of unconditional love. Loving others is effective in destroying racism. Dr. Martin Luther King, Jr. once said, "Darkness cannot drive out darkness, only light can do that. Hate cannot drive out hate, only love can do that."[63]

Loving unconditionally allows people to see beyond the surface. Differences are no longer highlighted and the reality that all people are image-bearers of God is spotlighted. Loving people moves the conversation beyond group stereotypes and acknowledges the individual. Unconditional love supplants the idea that all of a certain kind of people do certain things. That is just not true. They do not. Unconditional love provides a platform for honest, difficult discussions. Ministry across lines of difference, especially with respect to race, must be coated in unconditional love.

Be Patient

Paul writes, "love is patient" (1 Cor 13:4). The word he uses for patient is a word that means, "to suffer long or preserve." That attribute of love is important, especially when it comes to working across racial lines. According to Loritts, "Patience has been described as the refusal to make someone move at your pace."[64] This is a critical characteristic for those who minister across lines of difference.

In today's culture, there is a demand that people respond quickly when injustice occurs. Not only is public action or comment demanded, but there is often a call for punitive measures to be taken for those who do not see the issue the same way. This sentiment has led to a reactionary culture that demands instant agreement or else. While there is a right and wrong, it is not loving or helpful to adopt this "instant agreement" mentality. Patience allows people on both sides to take the time necessary to process and come to a just and right conclusion. Patience allows for the celebration of incremental success. Patience permits people to change their opinions on a particular event or topic as more information is obtained. Loritts

Who is My Neighbor?

maintains, "It takes patience to genuinely listen and seek not only to sympathize but to even offer an apology."[65] Listening to someone is an exercise of patience that is worth the effort. Allowing someone to share stories of pain and disappointment requires patience, but it makes a difference. Patience is invaluable in ministering effectively across lines of difference.

Why Does the Discussion of Race and Ethnicity Matter?

The evidence is clear, both scientifically and biblically, that there is only one race, the human race. The Bible does not define race the way our culture does. Despite biological and biblical arguments to the contrary, our culture views ethnicity and race as synonymous. Those who do ministry across lines of difference cannot.

The reality of there being one race, the human race is critical in understanding that all human beings are created in the image of God. There was no "primary" race or "first" race. There is no place for white supremacy or any other racial preference system. God created all humans to be one people. Baucham reasoned, "The concept of race is not a biblical concept, it's not a biblical idea, it is a constructed idea. You won't find the idea of races in the Bible unless you find it in the proper historical context where we see, number one, that we are all the race of Adam. Amen? One race, one blood. We are all the race of Adam. There is less than a 0.2 percent genetic difference between any of us in this regard."[66]

The fact that there is only the human race is critical for biblically combating racism and prejudice. Racism is a sin because it is making value judgments about people on external characteristics and traits that are perceived to be different. Biology has already made it clear that the differences in humans, from a DNA standpoint, are minuscule. Human beings are different shades of the same color. Humans are not as different as many want to say they are. There is no reason to differentiate based on differences that are insignificant.

That there is only one race, the human race, is also a unifying factor. Once the fact of one race is accepted, then humans can recognize their place and part in it. Human beings are in the same boat. Peter acknowledged this truth: "Then Peter began to speak: 'I now realize how true it is that God does not show favoritism but accepts from every nation the one who fears him and does what is right'" (Acts 10:34-35).

Methodology

Chapter 3

Authenticity

Effective ministry to the city is important. The components of effective ministry to city populations are found in the scriptures. Paul writes, "Love must be sincere. Hate what is evil; cling to what is good. Be devoted to one another in love. Honor one another above yourselves. Never be lacking in zeal, but keep your spiritual fervor, serving the Lord" (Rom 12:9-11). Paul's command can be summarized succinctly: Effective ministry to the city must be Authentic, Caring, Transformative, and Sustainable.

What Does Authentic Ministry Look Like?

Authenticity is necessary to reach diverse populations. Williams suggests that the harvest fields of inner-city America are yearning for authentic believers who are committed to bringing the message and touch of Jesus Christ to those who live there.[67] Authenticity is marked by a genuine walk with Jesus Christ. That is shown first by humility and the recognition that there is not one way to worship. People of diverse cultures may express praise, worship, and dedication differently. Authenticity recognizes the preferred approach of the one ministering but also respects the approaches of those being served. The second part of the definition is that authenticity is to journey with people, recognizing that the launch of a new ministry is not necessarily the first time God has been working in a particular place. Those who seek to minister to the city must acknowledge the ministry efforts already at work in the city. Those who minister effectively to diverse groups understand that they are the next link in a long chain of servants that God is using to expand his kingdom. The final component of authenticity with respect to ministry is that the minister is transparent in his or her own walk with Jesus. No one does the walk of faith perfectly other than Jesus Christ. There is no Savior other than Jesus. These three components of authenticity are vital if ministry across lines of difference is to be meaningful.

Benefits of Authentic Ministry

One of the benefits of an authentic ministry is that it builds trust. If people are to receive the message, they must trust the messenger. If they do not believe the person is authentic, the message will not convince or convict them.[68] This only makes sense. A message is only as trustworthy as the messenger. If those who minister across lines of difference are to make an impact, they must be heard and believed. How can they be heard if they, themselves, are not believable? Paul issues that challenge in Ephesians 4:25 as he writes, "Therefore each of you must put off falsehood and speak truthfully to your neighbor, for we are all members of one body."

Another benefit of authenticity is that it is tied to love. Authenticity is the vehicle through which love is shown. While adherence to the truth matters and right doctrine is vital, what authenticates our Christianity is not belief statements or convictions, but love.[69] Jesus said, "A new command I give you: Love one another. As I have loved you, so you must love one another. By this everyone will know you are my disciples if you love one another" (John 13:34-35). Authenticity demands a real relationship with Jesus Christ and requires loving and pouring into the lives of the people served. The people ministered to must know and see the love of those ministering. Authenticity is how the privilege to minister is earned. Authenticity is a crucial component of effective ministry to diverse communities of people and must be emphasized in the training of ministry students. Williams asserts, "In a world where all you have is your name, authenticity is priceless."[70] To understand authenticity with respect to ministry across lines of difference, three truths must be examined.

It's Not Your Way or the Highway

Authenticity demands a humble spirit in those who minister. Williams advised, "Whether you are called to share the gospel outside the ragged front door of a crack house in the 'hood' or with a new neighbor who just moved to town from another state, you are going to have to take some drastic steps to fit into their world, to understand them."[71] If ministry across lines of difference is to be effective, those ministering must take the time to know and learn about the people they serve. It won't work to implement a program without regard for how it will impact the people.

That's a Mistake

There is a scene in the 1951 movie *The African Queen* that stands out as an example of what is not effective in ministry across lines of difference. The movie, starring Humphrey Bogart and Katherine Hepburn, is well-known, but not for this scene. In the movie, well-meaning missionaries, played by Katherine Hepburn and Robert Morley, want to reach the natives in German East Africa in 1914 with the Good News. The scene is one in which the missionaries are leading a service that would have been appropriate in middle America, but woefully out of place in East Africa. The scene would be humorous if it wasn't so true. How many times do well-intentioned ministries attempt to reach across lines of difference and fail because they don't understand the people and culture they try to reach? Authenticity demands humility and understanding that your preferred approach to ministry, worship, or even how to "do church" is not the only correct one.

God is Reaching Out to All People

God is calling all people unto himself. Peter writes, "The Lord is not slow in keeping his promise, as some understand slowness. Instead, he is patient with you, not wanting anyone to perish, but everyone to come to repentance" (2 Peter 3:9). God's desire is for people of all ethnicities and backgrounds to come to him. Micah prophesied about this truth: "Many nations will come and say, 'Come, let us go up to the mountain of the Lord, to the temple of the God of Jacob. He will teach us his ways, so that we may walk in his paths'" (Micah 4:2). God intends for all people to worship him. "Among the gods there is none like you, Lord; no deeds can compare with yours. All the nations you have made will come and worship before you, Lord; they will bring glory to your name" (Psalm 86:8-9). The apostle Paul in Ephesians 2, observes the nature of the church: "For he himself is our peace, who has made the two groups one and has destroyed the barrier, the dividing wall of hostility, by setting aside in his flesh the law with its commands and regulations. His purpose was to create in himself one new humanity out of the two, thus making peace, and in one body to reconcile both of them to God through the cross, by which he put to death their hostility" (Ephesians 2:14-16). A. Skevington Wood writes about these verses, "The purpose of Christ, when he died on the cross, was not simply that Jews and Gentiles be reconciled to each other, but that both of them together should be reconciled to God."[72] At the cross, Jesus made the two diverse groups (Jew and Gentile) one. There is only one way to eternal life. All must go through Jesus. However, the way people praise Jesus can be different.

No One Right Way

Josh Davis and Nikki Lerner observe in their book *Worship Together in Your Church As in Heaven*, "God's desire is not that we have our own separate worship services suited to our individual tastes and preferences. God's desire is not that our congregations be unified around language or culture, a common mission, a cool brand, or a preferred musical style."[73] They assert, "God desires his people, from every nation, be unified around Jesus worshipping together."[74] That leads to an important question. What is the right approach when wanting to begin a ministry across lines of racial, cultural, or socio-economic difference?

First, observe how the people already worship the Lord. What kind of music is utilized in worship among that group? Are people more apt to express emotions during worship and praise times? Even if a new ministry is starting in an area, understanding how the people in that area think and express themselves is critical. Williams notes the ministry of Jamie, a short-term missionary in the inner city of Oakland, California. After an interview with her, Williams reports her perspective: "Entering into a community with the thought that you're going to start something doesn't respect what is going on in that community." She continues, "As an outsider, you don't really know anything yet…Actually, staying in that place where you feel as though you know very little is always a good place to stay in ministry-wise."[75] Coming into a ministry, especially across lines of difference with the notion this is the "correct way," will likely alienate those the ministry seeks to serve.

Second, categorize what are preferences and what are essentials. It is essential that all worship and praise goes to the Lord. The types and numbers of musical instruments are a preference. Biblically based preaching and teaching must be essential. The length of the sermon, the number and breakdown of the classes is a preference. Loving and respecting everyone in the body of Christ is an essential. Shaking hands, holy hugs, church dinners and fellowships are preferences. If an honest evaluation is done prayerfully and biblically, there will likely be more preferences than essentials.

Finally, commit to the big picture. The goal of the body of Christ is to worship and serve the Lord until he comes back. Those who serve in ministry are called by him. DeYmaz and Li ask a thought-provoking question: "Will you continue to entrust yourself and your family to a faithful Creator by going where he sends and doing what he calls you to do?"[76] Jesus said, "No one who puts a hand to the plow and looks back is fit for service in the kingdom of God" (Luke 9:62). The challenge is real for those who seek to minister across lines of difference. Understanding it's not your way or the highway is vital.

It Doesn't All Begin With You

Authenticity also demands the recognition that God's work doesn't necessarily start when a new ministry arrives. There is a tendency, especially in the United States, to value self-sufficiency and control of our own lives and destiny. DeYmaz observes this truth and counters, "Yet this is not how God would have us live. In fact, such a mind-set is contradictory to Christ-centered spiritual life. Rather, we are taught throughout the Bible to recognize, *There is a God, and I am not him.*"[77] Sometimes those in ministry see themselves as the start of God doing something.

I've heard the question asked in church staff meetings several times. I am sure it is well-intentioned, but I cringe every time I hear it. The question is, "If our church disappeared tomorrow, would anyone in the community realize we were gone?" Again, I understand

Who is My Neighbor?

what the question implies. It can be used as a springboard for a good discussion of how a church can become more community minded. What I have seen, though, is people ignore what a church has done for many years and operate under the assumption that God is, only now, beginning to work in this church. If ministry, especially across lines of difference, is to be effective, there needs to be a realization that God has likely already been at work where we are. Take some time, as was noted earlier, to see what he's been doing, and be humble in recognizing that your ministry is simply the next link in his chain. How do we do that? There are two important things to remember.

God's Plan for the Church is Ethnic Unity not just Diversity

The church cannot just settle for diversity. She must be committed to ethnic unity.[78] It is clear that God's desire is not for different ethnicities to simply acknowledge each other. His desire is for them to be one. Paul writes, "There is neither Jew nor Gentile, neither slave nor free, nor is there male and female, for *you are all one in Christ Jesus*" (Galatians 3:28, emphasis mine). For all to be "one in Christ" is not an easy thing.

One of the best ways to move from diversity to ethnic unity, according to Loritts, is socialization.[79] The reality is that many people do not think they have much in common with people of a different ethnicity. According to a Pew Research Center report from June 11, 2015, "Among those who are single-race white, 62% say they have a lot in common with people in the U.S. who are white, while about one-in-ten or fewer say they have a lot in common with people who are black, Asian, or American Indian. The pattern is similar for adults who are single-race black or Asian."[80] The data from that study is troubling, but adding to the problem is the fact that people do not seem to be able to talk about it. Melissa De Witte writes for *Stanford News:* "Researchers found that people view conversations with a friend about race as beneficial – they believe they can lead to better understanding, learning and closeness. But accompanying these positive expectations is a fear that these conversations could go badly." She continues, "Among white participants, some said they felt that they lacked a common ground on which to have these kinds of discussions. Others were scared they might say the wrong thing or come across as racist." She also wrote, "Black participants also saw possible pitfalls. They said they were more hesitant to talk about their race-related experiences with their white friends than they were with friends of color. They worried that their white friend might dismiss their experience, not understand them, or see them through the lens of a stereotype – even if inadvertently."[81] Despite the awkwardness of conversations, dialog and engagement is crucial if we, as Christians, are to get to ethnic unity. Socialization can emphasize humility.

What does socialization look like? How can it be done? Socialization is about relationships. It goes deeper than just having a friend of a different ethnicity. It means doing life with people of all ethnicities and backgrounds. This includes attending church together, serving the Lord together, having children go to the same schools, playing on the same teams and growing up in the same neighborhood. To do this well means people have to understand that not everyone sees every issue the same way and it has to be okay. Bryan Loritts calls this "Cultural Scripts." About this, he writes, "A cultural script is a way of seeing, living in, navigating the world, informed by a host of factors such as language, ethnicity, 'class and locale.'"[82] The cultural scripts that people carry with them can inhibit ministry across lines of difference and stifle moving from ethnic diversity to ethnic unity. Relationships help minimize the impact of cultural scripts. Knowing people on a personal level changes things. Differences melt away in the warmth of friendship.

Unity with Others Starts with Unity with Jesus

A second principle to understand when it comes to realizing it doesn't begin with you is that unity with others happens because of unity with Jesus Christ. When Jesus was asked by an expert in the law about what was the greatest commandment in the law, Jesus gave him a succinct answer: "Love the Lord your God with all your heart and with all your soul and with all your mind. This is the first and greatest commandment. And the second is like it: Love your neighbor as yourself. All the Law and the Prophets hang on these two commandments" (Matthew 22:37-40).

Who is My Neighbor?

The first part of Jesus' answer to the expert in the law goes back to Deuteronomy 6:4-5, which the Jews called the "Shema." They understood that there were to be no other gods but Yahweh and that he, and he alone, merited their love. The second part of his answer connects to what we call "The Golden Rule" (Matthew 7:12). Loving your neighbor as yourself is a challenge, to view other's needs and concerns as we would our own. Expressed most simply, it means a follower of Jesus does not say, "It's not my problem." A follower of Jesus is concerned about what is happening to his neighbor and cares about what happens to him.

Loving the Lord and loving our neighbor in this way is a catalyst for unity. When we recognize the oneness that we all share in Jesus Christ, it minimizes that which divides us. Loritts writes, "When we commit ourselves to loving God with the totality of our being and love others as ourselves, we are poised to experience ethnic unity."[83]

Ethnic unity is not easy. The church has struggled with it for a long time. The Jews in the Ephesian church had a hard time worshiping with Gentiles. The Jews, throughout their history, were God's chosen people. Being God's people was almost synonymous with being a Jew. It was incredibly difficult for them to understand that God's reach went beyond their ethnic group. In Ephesians 2, Paul reminds the Gentiles that at one time they were far from God, called the "uncircumcised," separate from Christ and without hope. Notice though, Ephesians 2:13, "But now in Christ Jesus you who once were far away have been brought near by the blood of Christ."

The key phrase in that wonderful verse is, ***in Christ Jesus.*** Because they chose to be ***in Christ Jesus,*** those who were once far away were brought near. Ethnic unity begins with being ***in Christ Jesus.*** There have been many attempts to create racial or ethnic harmony. Laws have been passed. Marches have been held. Campaigns have been organized. Some of these are well-intentioned. However, I am convinced that genuine ethnic unity cannot happen outside of Jesus Christ. Paul writes, "Just as a body, though one, has many parts, but all its many parts form one body, so it is with Christ. For we were all baptized by one Spirit so as to form one body—whether Jews or

Gentiles, slave or free—and we were all given the one Spirit to drink" (1 Cor 12:12-13).

No One's Perfect

Authenticity demands the recognition that no one is perfect. Those who seek to minister across lines of racial, cultural, and socio-economic differences must be transparent. There is a saying that has gained some traction in contemporary culture. Maybe you've heard it: "Fake it 'till you make it." The positive spin on this statement is that people who maybe lack self-confidence can develop it by just doing what they do and acting like they are assured and under control. Perhaps there is some benefit to this, but generally "faking it 'till you make it" is a recipe for disaster. It doesn't take long for people to realize that someone doing that is an imposter.

Most people probably don't remember the name George O'Leary. In December 2001 O'Leary was forced to resign his position as the head football coach at Notre Dame. He had not lost a game, nor were there any wild allegations of improper acts. Why was he forced to resign? He lied on his resume. He tried to pass off that he was something that he wasn't. From his days of playing football in college to earning a master's degree, O'Leary was trying to "fake it 'till he made it." At Notre Dame, one of the most scrutinized football programs in the country, O'Leary's deception was brought to light. What would have happened if O'Leary had been honest about who he was and what he'd done? He'd coached football pretty well at Georgia Tech before getting hired by Notre Dame. He might have been hired to coach football. However, trying to portray himself as something he wasn't left O'Leary out in the cold.

What happened to Coach O'Leary can happen to those in ministry. Authenticity in ministry demands that we are honest about who we are and where we are in our walk with Jesus Christ. In the early days of the church, the story of Ananias and Sapphira stands out as a cautionary tale. The story is a familiar one found in Acts 5. The church is new and growing. People, led by the Holy Spirit, are making contributions to help those in the community of believers. Ananias and Sapphira are a couple that has some property that they can sell to give to the cause. They agree to do it, but they secretly will hold back some of the money for themselves. They want to give the appearance of giving all, but in reality, they only give part. It doesn't go well. In fact, Peter confronts them, first Ananias and then his wife. He tells them they have lied to the Holy Spirit, and they fall down dead. The warning is clear. Don't pretend you are something you are not.

Don't Act Like the Expert

There is a temptation, when entering a new ministry situation, to act like the expert, the one who has it all together. If anything is to be learned from Coach O'Leary, or Ananias and Sapphira, it's don't do that. Be honest about who you are. Be honest about your own struggles. Be honest about your strengths and your weaknesses. What is needed to make an impact in this kind of ministry is willingness, compassion, and love. Williams remarked, "You don't need a graduate degree or ordination papers. You need compassion and a heart surrendered to Jesus Christ. I have met members of the resistance who change diapers in the church nursery, pick up children for Sunday School, mentor inner-city youth and hand out food in tent cities. Are you prepared to love as Jesus loved?"[84]

Success in ministry across lines of difference begins with a humble spirit. There are few experts when it comes to living out the faith the Lord desires for us, so don't try to act like one. We are simply "one beggar telling another beggar where to find bread." The origin of that quote is debated by many, but the truth of it is not. Those who do ministry across lines of racial, cultural, and socio-economic differences probably don't have all the answers. I know that I don't, and while there are many great books on the subject, I have yet to find one that has *the* answer to the ethnic disunity we see in the church. I am convinced, though, that a single answer will never be found. I believe there is no single answer. It seems to me to be a process. Those who approach the challenge of ethnic unity as a journey on which we are all fellow travelers will do better working with and serving all kinds of people.

Own Your Own Story

The other aspect of recognizing that no one is perfect is the importance of owning your own story. All Christians have areas of weakness. No one in ministry has a perfect spiritual life. Those who minister well across lines of difference are those who are honest about their own walk with Jesus. They are willing to share where it is strong and where it isn't. Paul writes, "For by the grace given me I say to every one of you: Do not think of yourself more highly than you ought, but rather think of yourself with sober judgment, in accordance with the faith God has distributed to each of you" (Romans 12:3). Paul, in the context of noting the various gifts in the Body of Christ, warns the Roman Christians about thinking too highly of themselves or having a super-spirituality.

How many ministries have faded into irrelevance because those leading it became convinced that they were the driving force behind it? "Pride goes before destruction, a haughty spirit before a fall" (Proverbs 16:18). A quick glance through social media sites reveals several stories of ministers who believed themselves to be bigger than the ministry. The church, the Bride of Christ, suffers when her leaders act as if they, themselves, are the savior. The church needs only one Savior. It isn't me or you. Owning our own story is crucial, and those leaders who do will gain the respect of those they seek to lead. They will not become targets of ambush for Satan or those who want to harm the church. Be who you are and be honest about it. Paul urges the Christians in Galatia, "If anyone thinks they are something when they are not, they deceive themselves. Each one should test their own actions. Then they can take pride in themselves alone, without comparing themselves to someone else, for each one should carry their own load" (Gal 6:3-5). These words are appropriate for those who minister today. Don't pretend you are something you're not. Be who you are.

Chapter 4

Caring

Effective ministry to diverse cultures must also reflect a caring attitude. Christians who have so much cannot refuse to help others who have so little (1 John 3:17). Williams posits a convicting question that is important for all Christians to consider: "If church members saw Jesus in the faces of the poor, would they do nothing?"[85] If Christians are to be effective, they cannot be indifferent to the needs of those around them. Christians reach out, serve, and love, because God reached out first.[86] The sheer number of people caught in the snare of poverty is astonishing. The task for Christians, especially in urban ministry, is seen in the Old Testament. "Speak up for those who cannot speak for themselves, for the rights of all who are destitute. Speak up and judge fairly; defend the rights of the poor and needy" (Prov 31:8-9). Christians must do this if they are to make a lasting difference.

Meeting the needs of those who are hurting or struggling is showing them the Lord Jesus Christ. Love for others flows from loving God. The New Testament demonstrates that a relationship with God is connected to relationships with others.[87] Caring about the struggle of those in the community demonstrates the fundamental truth that Jesus cares. A caring church can have an influence in the community. When there are healthy churches in urban areas, they become advocates for elevating the quality of life there.[88] Caring for the needs of the people is a foundational principle of a successful ministry to different people groups. Giving a cup of cold water to one who is thirsty may open the door to sharing living water with one whose thirst is eternal. This chapter addresses understanding what poverty is and what Christians need to do to help those in poverty.

What is Poverty?

Poverty is often defined as the human condition of being unable to obtain or provide a standard level of food, water and/or shelter for oneself or one's family.[89] However, from the point of view of a Christian, there is more to it. Steinman explained, "Poverty is about much more than what you can afford to do or buy. It is also about whether you feel part of society, and whether you can join in with other people."[90] This statement is critical to understanding what poverty is and how those in ministry can address it. God's view of how to treat those who are in need is clear: "For he will deliver the needy who cry out, the afflicted who have no one to help. He will take pity on the weak and the needy and save the needy from death. He will rescue them from oppression and violence, for precious is their blood in his sight" (Psalms 72:12-14). Jesus, himself, said, "Do not be afraid, little flock, for your Father has been pleased to give you the kingdom. Sell your possessions and give to the poor. Provide purses for yourselves that will not wear out, a treasure in heaven that will never fail, where no thief comes near, and no moth destroys. For where your treasure is, there your heart will be also" (Luke 12:32-34).

There are opportunities for Christians to minister to all kinds of people if they are open to it and aware of what is going on around them. Bill Fay notes in his study for *Debt.org* that the highest poverty rate on record was 22% in the 1950's and was at an all-time low in 2019, before the pandemic, at 10.5%.[91] However, according to the U.S. Census in 2022, the poverty rate was up to 12.4% or almost 38 million people in poverty.[92] The poverty numbers vacillate, but the number of people who struggle with it is an alarming statistic. There are many people in the United States who do not have the means to take care of their needs in the culture in which we live. God intends for his people to minister to the poor and demonstrate the love of Jesus to them.

Where I've Seen Poverty

I served a church in Kansas City, Kansas, from the mid-1990's until 2009. Kansas City, Kansas, was becoming an urban area at that time, and we dealt with people in our community who were poor.

Methodology   Chapter 4

This was the reality for our church. I was also privileged to take two mission trips to Tijuana with a group from our church in the summers of 2007 and 2008, along with an organization that built homes for those who did not have them. This, too, was an opportunity to work with those who had little.

The people we served in these experiences were in need. They were lacking food, money for rent, transportation, funds for medicine, and many of them had a general inability to acquire basic needs. At the Kansas City church, we had a benevolent fund which we used to meet the needs of those struggling in the church and in the community. That fund was called on multiple times a month throughout my ministry in Kansas City. Our church helped many people pay utility bills, rent, and buy groceries. We also had a food pantry that distributed food. We distributed grocery bags to people in need in our community and when the pantry was empty, we had a food drive. In addition to the food pantry at our church, we worked in a downtown Kansas City, Kansas, food kitchen once a month. There we would provide a meal for over three hundred people at a time. Our church was located in what was becoming an urban area. We wanted to do all we could to make a difference.

The mission trips were short-term experiences, but both times our group worked hard to construct houses for families who needed them. During our two mission trips, we built three different houses in different areas of the city. There were times when we saw firsthand, the depths of poverty. We were blessed to be able to help and share with them.

Looking back, I see some positives from those experiences. I worked with a lot of people who genuinely cared for others and wanted to help them. There were also people who looked beyond themselves to see how they could serve God by making a difference. Those with whom I served gave with the best motives and intentions. Similarities are notable in all these ministry encounters. First, in both of these situations, people had needs that were greater than their resources. They could not exist and live like the rest of the people around them unless these needs were addressed. Second, the group I worked with handled the needs. We did what we could to make a difference. It is important to note that we did not have the people we were helping, engage in the ministry we were doing. It was something we did for them. Third, the people that we helped were usually grateful, but largely unknown to us who helped them. While I think the ways we helped and served those in need were at some level successful, looking back, I sense we could have done some things better.

Is There A Better Way?

While I am grateful for the opportunities to have served those in need, I am convinced there are things I can do better. There are two principles that ought to serve as a foundation for ministry across lines of difference.

First, it is important to recognize the greatest need. In many cases, the most important thing is not having sustenance for the moment, but to acquire the ability to obtain one's own needs. In many cases, we saw the same people coming each month for food or an electric bill. We were providing a temporary fix for them, but we did not do as much as we could to alleviate the larger problem. A better way to help them overall would have been to assist them in getting employment. The ancient proverb is true. "Give a man a fish, and you feed him for a day. Teach a man to fish, and you feed him for a lifetime." Ministries such as the Greensboro Urban Ministry Center in Greensboro, North Carolina, work together with other ministries and community leaders to help people find employment. They embody that truth that "finding a job and building a sustainable career is the fastest and most viable way to improve your standard of living."[93] Successful ministries across lines of difference will help people help themselves. Equipping and enabling people to provide for themselves and their families is a blessing to them. Paul challenged Timothy: "Anyone who does not provide for their relatives, and especially for their own household, has denied the faith and is worse than an unbeliever" (1 Tim 5:8). We do well to help those in need. We do even better to equip them to help themselves.

How can we do that? Those who provide food for the needy can change the way that they do it. Instead of offering free groceries at a certain time, allow a family or an individual to get the assistance for free for a limited time, but assist them in filling out job applications and submitting them. Bring potential employers to the site where the people who need jobs can meet with them.

Another option is to create a "discount grocery store." Instead of giving out free food, collect all the food to be distributed and allow people to come, once a month or so, to shop for themselves at discounted prices. People who purchase their own groceries and even pay discounted prices are doing more to "provide for themselves." For those who cannot afford even the discounted prices, allow them to work in the store to earn the money to purchase their items. Those who serve in these kinds of ministries have the opportunity to focus on not just meeting the immediate need but aiming to address the long-term problem. This approach is helping people while allowing them to retain their dignity. In their book, *When Helping Hurts,* Corbett and Fikkert claimed, "One of the biggest problems in many poverty-alleviation efforts is that their design and implementation exacerbates the poverty of being of the economically rich—their god-complexes—and the poverty of being of the economically poor—their feelings of inferiority and shame."[94] This is a crucial facet of ministry that goes unnoticed far too often. Jesus said, "So in everything, do to others what you would have them do to you, for this sums up the Law and the Prophets" (Matt. 7:12). To accomplish this, Christians have to move beyond just a "helping in the moment" mindset. It is not enough to give someone what they lack or pay a bill that needs to be paid. If followers of Jesus really want to help them as Jesus would (and as they, themselves, would want to be helped), they will do so in a way that allows them to keep or regain dignity and worth. Allowing them to pay the bill involves trusting that they will do it but has far more impact. Providing ways that income can be earned and then appropriately spent can be invaluable. Few, I believe, like getting a handout. It feels awkward and embarrassing. If it feels like that to me, it probably does to others, too.

A second principle that is important for Christians to consider as they minister to those in poverty is to view the purpose of the church in a broader context. The message of Jesus, while primarily about salvation, is not exclusively about eternity and what comes next. It is also about what is happening now. "Converts need to be trained in a biblical worldview that understands the implications of Christ's lordship for all of life and that seeks to answer the question: If Christ is Lord of all, how do we do farming, business, government, family, art, etc., to the glory of God?"[95] This should not minimize the importance of salvation. That remains the primary task of the church. However, it is also true that a Christian, once he knows Jesus Christ, cannot help but want to impact the community around him.

While I believe the church knows and understands this, there are times when she neglects the "here and now." It is important that our churches and schools, especially evangelical churches and schools, be concerned how Jesus is made visible in daily life. Are people seeing Jesus in how Christians address real issues and problems that people face? Corbett and Fikkert assert there are "both a now and a not yet" to the kingdom."[96] Additionally, they contend that many evangelical Christians answer the question about why Jesus came, with statements referring to his death on the cross, resurrection and redemption. Again, this was Jesus' primary purpose and there is no dispute about that. However, Corbett and Fikkert argue that "Jesus preached the good news of the kingdom in word and in deed, so the church must do the same."[97] Salvation and eternity in heaven is a part of the Kingdom message, a big part, but not the whole of it. "Personal piety and formal worship are essential to the Christian life, but it must lead to lives that act justly and love mercy," say Corbett and Fikkert.[98] Their summary is succinct. "When people look at the church, they should see the One who declared—in word and in deed to the leper, the lame, and the poor—that His kingdom is bringing healing to every speck of the universe."[99]

The Bible is clear that Jesus was concerned for the poor. While teaching in the synagogue, Jesus stood to read the scriptures and was handed the book of Isaiah. He announced that he was sent to proclaim the good news to the poor (Luke 4:18). A woman who had been severely bleeding for twelve years came to Jesus. Her illness had left her destitute. She spent all she had to find a cure, but to no avail. Jesus stopped a procession to the house of the synagogue ruler to reach out to this anonymous woman (Luke 8:43-48). Jesus taught that membership in his kingdom did not depend upon the amount of material goods someone possessed.

Methodology   Chapter 4

Process to Combat Poverty

For making disciples in cities and in areas that are struggling with poverty, there must be a commitment to the biblical imperative that compels Christians to reach the lost. Jesus said, "The harvest is plentiful, but the workers are few. Ask the Lord of the harvest, therefore, to send out workers into his harvest field" (Matt 9:37-38). There are three critical steps involved in this process.

The first step in making disciples in areas wrestling with poverty is to have compassion for the people there. Williams commented, "When Jesus experienced compassion, he was moved in his guts, in the very core of his being, by the plight of the person in front of him. When Jesus was filled with compassion, he responded with all of his power to meet the need."[100] That is a challenge that Christians must meet if there is to be effective outreach across lines of difference with respect to poverty. Poverty is widespread in many places around the world. "And nowhere is poverty more visible than in the slums and shantytowns that spread out from the edges of Lima or Bangkok."[101] John Fuder poses relevant questions: "When we walk down the streets of our cities, when we drive through the neglected, despairing, destitute neighborhoods, when we see crowds of people, how do we respond? How deeply do we see? Are we moved to compassion or revulsion?"[102] Compassion is more than just a feeling. It must be an action. "If one of you says to them, 'Go in peace; keep warm and well fed,' but does nothing about their physical needs, what good is it?" (James 2:16).

The second step to making disciples in places where poverty is widespread is to have a sustainable presence in the area. Conn and Ortiz ask an important question. "Urban populations will continue to grow at almost twice the rate of national growth, and large cities at a rate three to four times as high. Does the church show any indication of interest in these expanding urban centers?[103] The answer to this question must be yes. Mark Gornik and Maria Liu Wong note, "When we stay in the city, we don't know what God will do, what we will see afresh or encounter. But God has invited all of us to stay in the city, to wait to receive power from on high, the gift of the Spirit, and to trust how God is already at work."[104] Successful, disciple-making ministries in urban areas must maintain a presence. Paul ministered in the city of Ephesus for two years (Acts 19:1-12). That is a valuable example.

The third step is to emphasize connections. Jesus' ministry focused on connections. He came to connect people to the Father and to each other. He connected with others, especially those on the fringes of society, to meet their needs and demonstrate love and compassion. Paul writes, "He came and preached peace to you who were far away and peace to those who were near. For through him we both have access to the Father by one Spirit" (Eph 2:17-18). Jesus came to connect diverse people to God and to each other. Connecting was at the heart of Jesus' ministry and needs to be at the heart of our ministries.

Summing Up

The writer of Hebrews, looking ahead to the eternal city and recognizing the Christian's responsibility here, says, "For here we do not have an enduring city, but we are looking for the city that is to come. Through Jesus, therefore, let us continually offer to God a sacrifice of praise—the fruit of lips that openly profess his name. And do not forget to do good and to share with others, for with such sacrifices God is pleased" (Heb 13:14-16). While we await the eternal city, we are to do good in the cities in which we live. Christians are to live for Jesus in ways that make a real impact, not just in the future but now. "Suppose a brother or a sister is without clothes and daily food. If one of you says to them, "Go in peace; keep warm and well fed," but does nothing about their physical needs, what good is it? In the same way, faith by itself, if it is not accompanied by action, is dead" (James 2:15-17). I believe this is a powerful point that needs to be lived out in all our ministries.

Christians must be known as caring people. Too many times, in today's culture, Christians are perceived to be judgmental, critical, and sometimes hateful. I believe these characterizations are not accurate for the majority of the body of Christ. However, there are times when the church has missed an opportunity to demonstrate kindness and caring. The Body of Christ, on occasion, has been indifferent to hurting people, allowing those on the radical fringe (think Westboro Baptist of Topeka, Kansas) to define the Christian response. The church is not defined or summarized by Westboro Baptist and those like them. However, when we fail to do right, our culture assigns the "Christian view" to people who do not represent it. Those who know the right thing to do and don't do it, that is sin (James 4:17).

Again, there is a caution to be heeded. Simply performing caring acts is not the totality of the Christian response. The "social gospel" is no gospel at all if it does not point to Jesus. If salvation in Jesus Christ is not at the center of our message, we have the wrong message. Having noted that, if all we do is discuss the "sweet by and by" and never address present concerns, do we really teach the gospel? I wonder sometimes, how many Christians pass by those hurting without noticing or seeing them? Do I see hurting people today? Effective ministries, like the Samaritan, see themselves as the neighbor of the one in need (Luke 10:36-37). Timothy Keller writes of the importance of deeds in connection with the gospel: "Because the gospel is presented to the world not only through word but also through deed and community, we should not choose between teaching and carrying out practical ministry to address people's needs."[105] There is no doubt the gospel must point to Jesus. That is not a point of discussion. However, a gospel that does not minister to people in the struggles of this life is not really the gospel message either and does nothing to demonstrate Jesus or faith (James 2:16). Caring, demonstrated through thoughtful acts of kindness, provides a path for which the gospel can be preached and taught.

Chapter 5

Transformation

Ministry to those of different cultures, backgrounds, and statuses must be transformative. It is important that authenticity and caring are the foundation of this kind of ministry. However, if the heart of this ministry is not transformation, it has no eternal significance. The gospel message changes the hearts and lives of all people. Effective ministry to diverse people groups must proclaim the cross of Christ and a personal relationship with Jesus. Nothing is more important than this message. Jesus' sacrifice paid the price for sin for all humanity. There is no discrimination, and there are no exceptions. In the ultimate act of love, Jesus brought life, hope, and healing, through his death and resurrection. He restored the relationship broken by sin. Jesus did not discriminate, and the cross does not discriminate.[106] Ministry to those who come from different cultures, socio-economic statuses, and races must not minimize what is the single, greatest unifying factor. Jesus Christ came to redeem all people and to bring them into a relationship with God through himself. Paul writes, "Do not conform to the pattern of this world but be transformed by the renewing of your mind. Then you will be able to test and approve what God's will is—his good, pleasing, and perfect will" (Rom 12:2). He adds, "Therefore, if anyone is in Christ, the new creation has come: The old has gone, the new is here" (2 Cor 5:17). New life is found in Jesus. One of the key components of transformation or having a relationship with God through Jesus Christ is reconciliation. Reconciliation, with respect to ministering across lines of differences, can be seen in two different ways.

Reconciliation with God

Transformation is what makes this kind of ministry distinctively Christian. One of the most significant outcomes of a transformed life is reconciliation. God gave Christians, through Jesus Christ, the ministry of reconciliation (2 Cor 5:18). There are two areas of life in which reconciliation must be prevalent. The first is reconciliation with God. Paul notes that "all have sinned and fall short of the glory of God" (Rom 3:23). All humanity has missed the mark. There is not one person who does not need a Savior. "For God so loved the world that he gave his one and only Son, that whoever believes in him shall not perish but have eternal life" (John 3:16). Preaching and teaching reconciliation to God through Jesus is critical for any ministry, including ministry across lines of racial, cultural, and socio-economic difference. The simple truth is all people need Jesus. Murray J. Harris writes, "Reconciliation is the divine act by which, on the basis of the death of Christ, God's holy displeasure against sinful man was appeased, the enmity between God and man was removed, and man was restored to proper relations with God."[107] Reconciliation with God matters.

Paul notes the significance of being reconciled to God in his second letter to the church at Corinth. 2 Corinthians 5:14-21 indicates the importance of this kind of reconciliation, and a close examination of this passage will provide a basis for understanding both aspects of reconciliation. Verses 14-15 indicate the basis for reconciliation. Jesus Christ died for all. Colin Kruse reasoned, "It was not the bare fact of Christ's death on the cross that moved Paul, it was the death of Christ understood in a particular way. It was his death for all."[108] Jesus' death is the foundation of reconciliation. It was his death that atoned for sin and paid the debt that sinners incurred. Verse 15 then provides an important ramification of Jesus' death: "And he died for all, that those who live should no longer live for themselves but for him who died for them and was raised again" (2 Cor 5:15). When human beings recognize that Jesus died for them to give them life, they are compelled to live for him and not for themselves. Receiving the reconciliation that Jesus' death offers, provides the opportunity for a person to have a new purpose for living. That is reiterated in verse 17: "If anyone is in Christ, the new creation has come. The old has gone and the new is here." Kruse observes, "The participation of the new creation is reflected in the new outlook of which verse 16 spoke, and in a new holiness of life."[109] For the person who knows Jesus Christ as Savior, life's purpose is to be like Jesus. Obviously, this refers to one's personal life. Christians need to grow in their walk with Jesus. However, being like Jesus is not just seen in personal conduct. Reconciliation to God through Jesus should impact how Christians view others and the world around them. A person who has been reconciled to God through Jesus Christ has a new outlook on life. Paul wrote, "and he has committed to us the message of reconciliation" (2 Cor 5:19). He adds that we are "Christ's ambassadors" (2 Cor 5:20), which indicates that all Christians are to reflect the kingdom of Christ in their lives. "God has not only reconciled the world to himself, but he has also commissioned messengers to proclaim that good news."[110]

Concerns About Understanding Reconciliation

Do Christians understand that being reconciled to God has broader implications than just one's personal life? There are some who would answer that question with a resounding, "no." Brenda Salter McNeil contends, "The gospel was always intended to transform groups of people and to empower them to confront larger spiritual forces. However, because white Americans' understanding of sin and transformation is highly individualistic, we have often remained powerless and silent before the greatest spirits of the age."[111] Bryan Loritts argues, "Individualistic discipleship in the Western world is not the kind of discipleship Jesus envisioned." He continues that discipleship values "the communal far more than Western culture does."[112] McNeil suggests, "Christ is more important than our racial or ethnic identities. This does not cancel or dismiss our cultural identity; it simply supersedes them as the most significant."[113]

Reconciliation with God matters. I will not minimize one's personal relationship to God through Jesus. However, it does seem that the Bible makes it clear that being reconciled to God not only impacts one's eternity but also influences one's "here and now." A Christian should have the same passion for pursuing justice and mercy (Micah 6:8) as they do for personal growth and piety (Eph 4:22-24). True reconciliation is not only the forgiveness of sins and the removal of guilt. Reconciliation is the receiving of God's gift of salvation and the accompanying gift of the Holy Spirit.[114] It is through the leading of the Holy Spirit that living out the Christian faith is possible. The path leading to harmonious relationships between people of divergent backgrounds and cultures must pass by the cross. Reconciliation with God empowers reconciliation to others.

Reconciliation with Others

Reconciliation with a diverse group of other people is not an easy thing. There have been multiple attempts in culture to bring people together. I was part of one such attempt growing up in Kansas City, Kansas. In 1978, Sumner High School, the predominantly black high school in downtown Kansas City, Kansas, was closed as a result of a court order to desegregate the KCK public school system. Sumner High School had been serving the community in Northeast Kansas City, Kansas since 1905. Sumner High School was changed to Sumner Academy of Arts and Science. It became a magnet school for highly motivated and academically talented students across the city. Students of that community who did not qualify for the new Sumner Academy were then bused to other high schools throughout Kansas City, Kansas. The plan, like many others in that period of history, was to use school busing to integrate schools and bring people of different backgrounds and cultures together.

Looking back on my high school experience, I am confident that I received a quality education, and I had friends of different backgrounds. On a micro level, I believe that the creation of Sumner Academy benefited me. However, I am not so sure it benefited the community on a macro level. First, the northeast community, which for many years celebrated the success of Sumner High School and viewed it as their own, lost a part of their identity. The history and success of Sumner High School were relegated to obscure pages on the Internet. Second, while the students at Sumner Academy came together across lines of difference, the community did not really unify. Most of the other schools joined in their dislike of Sumner Academy and its students. I experienced a few incidents personally. It was not a good time. From my experience, I believe the idea of destroying neighborhood schools in the name of racial reconciliation is not good.

The Relational Model

In many ways, I think the architects of the busing plans were attempting to address reconciliation through what is sometimes called "The Relational Model." The idea behind this model is to have people make friends with other people of different cultures and backgrounds. Then, one relationship at a time, change occurs. This model does have some strengths. It is not overly complicated and anyone with the desire to do it can do it. It is also something that a person can do on his/her own – it is a personal thing. While it does have some positive attributes, it should not be the only method Christians employ. "The friendship model does not bring adequate spiritual resources to bear on the immense problems of injustice, rage, guilt, shame and deep woundedness."[115] The "Relational Model" can bring individuals together but does not address the issues that divide different groups.

The Institutional Change Approach

A second approach to reconciliation is referred to as "The Institutional Change Approach." This method seeks to create justice and equality by redistributing power among groups. On the benign side of this approach, the goal is to bring more people from diverse backgrounds into an organization. The intent is to have a diversity of voices and faces at the higher levels of a group that will create an environment for reconciliation and working together. There is another side to the Institutional Change Model. As I see it, on the more troubling side of this approach is the view rooted in Marxism, which advocates for the oppressed to overthrow the oppressor and then become the oppressor. There are clear problems with this point of view from a Christian viewpoint. It reduces the purpose of all human relationships to a power paradigm. This model makes relationships competitive and pits people of difference against one another. With respect to reconciling people to each other, "The Institutional Change Model is not adequate to accomplish that because it does not address the transformation of the human heart."[116] Like "The Relational Model," "The Institutional Change Model" is not sufficient to ignite reconciliation among people.

What Approach Will Work?

Transformation is a critical component of successful ministry across lines of racial, cultural, and socio-economic differences. Reconciliation is a big part of transformation. Christians have the ministry and message of reconciliation, which involves personal reconciliation with God, but it is also on a horizontal plane, reconciliation with others. There are quite a few approaches that have been tried, and for a variety of reasons have not succeeded. What might be effective? I suggest a two-pronged approach. Reconciliation with others requires walking with Jesus led by the Holy Spirit and a commitment to discipleship.

Walking With Jesus, Led by the Holy Spirit

In my view, reconciliation cannot be done apart from a walk with Jesus. Clearly, this applies to reconciliation with God, but also with others. The Holy Spirit prompts and empowers Christians to live like Jesus. That includes loving and respecting others, standing for truth, and extending grace. Paul writes, "So I say, walk by the Spirit, and you will not gratify the desires of the flesh. For the flesh desires what is contrary to the Spirit, and the Spirit what is contrary to the flesh" (Gal 5:16-17). Jesus notes, "But when he, the Spirit of Truth comes, he will guide you into all the truth" (John 16:13). The indwelling of the Holy Spirit enables men and women of faith to live and act like Jesus. That is important in the discussion of reconciling people of different backgrounds and experiences. What does it look like to allow the Holy Spirit to work in a believer's life? With respect to reconciliation to others, there are four things, I believe, the Holy Spirit can empower and embolden Christians to do.

Be Honest About Other People's Identity

The first challenge is to be honest about those around us. There is a tendency among many, especially in the culture of our day, to categorize people and highlight what makes them different. This is being written during the election season, and multiple news media outlets are reporting who Black voters, Hispanic voters and women are supporting in the 2024 presidential election. Culture tends to divide entertainment and music by ethnic groups. Unfortunately, churches are often divided by ethnicity as well. There are Black churches, Hispanic churches, white churches, and many others. It is important to acknowledge, as has been previously done in this book, that there is only one race. People have much more in common with each other than they are different.

Understanding that is important, but it can lead to a different problem, a problem George Yancey calls, "colorblindness." He writes, "I have often heard whites talk about how they don't see color. I have talked to enough whites to understand the sentiment behind such assertions…However, I know how tone-deaf this statement comes across to many people of color. To say our race does not matter flies in the face of our life experience. To say you do not see that is to say you do not see an important aspect of my identity."[117] He suggests that to ignore a person's ethnicity is to ignore a part of the person him/herself.[118] Colorblindness, in theory, makes sense, after all, dividing people by superficial differences is wrong. However, in practice it denies an evident part of who a person is and rejects the creativity God used in creating them. The different ethnicities that populate the earth reflect the wonderful, diverse, creative nature of God. Seeing the different ethnicities of people allows us to celebrate the unique ways that people love, respond, and worship. To force a sense of "sameness" on all people stifles energy and enthusiasm. When I think about this, I am reminded of an episode of the old television show "The Twilight Zone." Do you remember Rod Serling's masterpiece? The episode that came to mind was the one called, "Number 12 Looks Just Like You." In that episode, all nineteen-year-olds went through a medical process in which they could choose one of about three or four choices for body type and looks. The society, in this "twilight zone," valued everyone being the same. It is a thoughtful, powerful episode.

While defining and categorizing people based on superficial differences is repugnant, refusing to acknowledge any difference among people is also dangerous. What is needed is a healthy balance. Celebrate difference without making it a dividing issue. This is what the Holy Spirit can lead the Christian to do. If we are to see reconciliation, we must begin to see people and be honest about them. At our core, we are the same, but we can celebrate the unique things each ethnicity brings to the table.

Be Sensitive to What is Going On Around You

Paul writes, "Do nothing out of selfish ambition or vain conceit. Rather, in humility, value others above yourselves, not looking to your own interests but each of you to the interests of others" (Phil 2:3-4). If we are to minister successfully across lines of difference and help bring about reconciliation, we will need to be aware of what is happening in other people's lives. How many times have we heard the sermon illustration that describes a person who has been attacked and is lying on the street only to have none of those in the neighborhood see what happened. While that story is told in many different variations, the reality is painfully true. Too many people do not choose to see or get involved in the lives of those around them. It is as if people are invisible.

In Ralph Ellison's 1952 story, "Invisible Man," the protagonist says, "I am invisible, understand, simply because people refuse to see me." That's a profound statement. He is invisible because people refuse to see him. Homelessness might not directly affect your family. Is it then, not real to you? You may not know a young person with a same-sex attraction. Does that mean same-sex attractions are no big deal? You may never face a situation of profiling or misconduct by law enforcement. Does that mean that it doesn't exist? Just because something is not our reality does not mean it isn't someone else's reality. Caring about what happens to others is critical in ministering, especially across lines of difference. Caring is what brings people of diverse backgrounds to the same place. Don't walk with Jesus with blinders on. See what he sees. Care about the things that break his heart. Doing that can help bring us all together.

Be Bold to Speak About Issues that Should Be Addressed

"If anyone, then, knows the good they ought to do and doesn't do it, it is sin for them" (James 4:17). Helping bring people together sometimes involves getting out of a comfort zone and speaking up about things that are wrong. Doing this is not easy, but it is important. The "good we ought to do" is sometimes standing up for those who are being mistreated.

The Holocaust Encyclopedia calls those who stood by while the holocaust was happening "bystanders." It notes that the term included those who did not speak out when they witnessed the persecution of individuals targeted simply because they were Jewish. I read about a tragic event that occurred in Florida. During the summer of 2017, a group of teens watched a man drown in a pond and did nothing but record it on their cell phones. Authorities reported that there was little to charge the teens with because there isn't a law in Florida that requires people to call for help for anyone in distress. Only a few states have these "Good Samaritan" laws.[119]

It is tough to imagine either of these things. How can people stand by and do nothing while an ethnic group is persecuted and killed? How can a group of kids just watch a man drown in a pond? These things ought not be. People should stand up for other people. I agree and might shout "Amen" a bit louder if I wasn't guilty of doing that sometimes. I have not stood by while people in front of me were apprehended and hauled off to concentration camps. I have not just watched while someone drowned. However, how many times have I heard an inappropriate joke that mocks an ethnicity or gender and simply turned away? How many times have I let people around me denigrate others without saying a word? How many times have I brought up a prayer request that impacted a different group of people? When was the last time I stood in the gap for someone who wasn't like me? We are called upon to do good. In fact, when we know the good we are to do and don't do it, that's sin. Having the boldness to speak and act in the face of injustice and not being a "bystander" will facilitate people coming together.

Demonstrate Compassion to those who have been Hurt

"Therefore, as God's chosen people, holy and dearly loved, clothe yourselves with compassion, kindness, humility, gentleness, and patience" (Col 3:12). The Greek words used for "compassion" in this verse are *splanchna* and *oiktirmou*. These words imply a deep, heartfelt caring that comes from deep within a person. Paul urges the

Christians in Colossae to put on compassion. For followers of Jesus, caring deeply about the misfortune and hurt of others ought to be in the DNA of the soul. Jesus said, "By this everyone will know that you are my disciples, if you love one another" (John 13:35).

What does demonstrating compassion to those who are hurting look like? As I see it, showing compassion to those who are hurting recognizes that I consider the plight of others my concern. When the child of a single parent is having trouble in my neighborhood, I do not respond, "Well, he's not my child." When the family on the other end of the street wrestles with storm damage, I don't say, "Glad it isn't my house." When the kids in my neighborhood school don't have enough supplies or books, my response isn't, "Well, that's not my problem." Compassion, for the Christian, recognizes that the problems of the people around me are my problems. I will care for them and do all I can to assist those in need. Too many times, Christians have been criticized as people who don't care about those who are not a part of their tribe. Shoveling the driveway of the same-sex couple in your neighborhood or cutting their grass is not making a statement about their union. It is simply saying, "I'm your neighbor. I see you as people and I care." We, in the Body of Christ, need to reclaim the badge of compassion. We ought to be known as the most compassionate people. Jesus is the most compassionate person to ever live. Shouldn't we be like him?

Commitment to Discipleship

The second component of this two-part approach is to be committed to discipleship. Reconciliation depends on allowing the Holy Spirit to be present in the four areas that were cited earlier and for Christians to be "all in" with respect to being like Jesus. Bryan Loritts writes, "It's time the church of Jesus Christ stops reacting to the problem of race and instead lead proactively by discipling people into the new humanity."[120] What does this commitment to discipleship look like? As I see it, there are two major components. A follower of Jesus must want to become more like Jesus, inwardly and outwardly. Second, a Christian man or woman needs to see his/her walk, not just personally, but in the context of community.

Methodology   Chapter 5

The Want To

Former North Carolina and Kansas basketball coach Roy Williams is known among coaches for talking about a team's "want-to." In describing a 2013 win over then, number one ranked Michigan State, Williams said, "Today, Michigan State did not want it that much more than we did. I think the want-to is always something that has been extremely important to me."[121] Coach Williams' "want-to" is the desire or passion to compel people, in his case basketball players, to go beyond what they think they can to attain the goal. If Christians are to make a difference in the reconciliation of diverse people groups, there will need to be a "want to" be like Jesus in every area of life. "Unity is only possible when we strive for something beyond us to bring us together."[122]

The desire to be more like Jesus and pursuing discipleship as a means of engaging in ministry across lines of racial, cultural, and socio-economic differences will create a better environment for lasting change. Paul describes it well as he writes, "And we all, who with unveiled faces contemplate the Lord's glory, are being transformed into his image with ever-increasing glory, which comes from the Lord who is the Spirit" (2 Cor 3:18).

Community: Something Bigger than Me

"Reconciliation is at the core of the gospel and is vital for the healing of people, and the healing of nations."[123] The gospel has the power to transform lives and communities. In many conservative churches, there is a commitment to teach and preach that the gospel reconciles an individual to God. That is vital, as we have already noted. However, there is a need for us to see the gospel can bind diverse groups of people together. "When we commit ourselves to loving God with the totality of our being and loving others as ourselves, we are poised to experience ethnic unity."[124] Paul urged the multi-ethnic church at Ephesus to "Make every effort to keep the unity of the Spirit through the bond of peace. There is one body and one Spirit, just as you were called to one hope when you were called" (Eph 4:3-4).

Who is My Neighbor?

Seeing our walk with Jesus as impacting more than our personal lives allows us the opportunity to make a difference with respect to reconciliation. Being a Christian is much more than just a personal thing. A Christian has joined a larger community of like-minded brothers and sisters who have much more reason to unite than they have to divide. May we do as Jesus prayed; be one as he and the Father are one.

Chapter 6

Sustainability

Ministry that impacts diverse communities is built on the foundation of authenticity and caring. Its passion is transformation, and its strength is sustainability. Simply put, effective ministry in areas of diversity must endure. Presence matters. The gospels record that many interactions and miracles happen because Jesus encounters people at precisely the right time. He is where the people are. That is what is effective.[125] There is no shortcut or substitute for consistently being there and involved in a ministry. Showing up is an important value for ministries that want to be successful. Those who lead successful ministries to people of diverse backgrounds must be committed to being there and doing the hard work to continue to develop and grow the ministry. Many ministries, especially in urban areas or across cultural lines, are there for just a season and are gone. Continued presence leads to continued results and growth, and this is to be the goal of effective ministry across lines of racial, cultural, and socio-economic difference.

What is Sustainability?

The Merriam-Webster Dictionary defines sustainable as "of, or relating to, or being a method of harvesting or using a resource that is not depleted or permanently damaged."[126] Sustainable ministry to those across lines of difference then, is a ministry or ministry process that will not be depleted. Sustainable ministry is one that is in it for the long haul. Those whose ministry is sustainable are those who are willing to leave a comfort zone and not look back. Jesus described such a person: "No one who puts a hand to the plow and looks back is fit for service in the kingdom of God" (Luke 9:62). Loritts notes, "There is a cost to leadership." He notes what is required for this kind of ministry; vulnerability and courage.[127] Put in the simplest terms I

Who is My Neighbor?

know, those who want to engage in sustainable ministry across lines of difference must be willing to go the distance.

In the first *Rocky* movie (1976), Sylvester Stallone plays the fighter Rocky Balboa. Rocky is just another Philadelphia fighter. He wins and loses fights and makes most of his money as a debt collector. The World Champion Apollo Creed visits Philadelphia and decides to give a local fighter a chance to fight him in an exhibition match. Rocky is randomly chosen. No one believes he can win or even survive more than a round or two. Rocky though, sees it differently. There is something down deep inside of him that rejects that prediction. In what has become a memorable quote, Balboa said he took the fight, "'Cause all I wanna do is go the distance. Nobody's ever gone the distance with Creed, and if I can go that distance, you see, and that bell rings and I'm still standin', I'm gonna know for the first time in my life, see, that I weren't just another bum from the neighborhood."

There is something inspiring and powerful about being willing to "go the distance." Ministry that is ultimately to be successful is built on a foundation of determination and persistence. In addition to staying the course, sustainable ministry is not willing to give up. Quitting is not an option for those who seek a sustainable ministry. Before we go too far, let's address an important issue. There are times when it is right for a ministry to conclude. There is quite a bit of material out there detailing how and when a ministry ought to end, and that topic is beyond the scope of this book. For our purposes, sustainable ministry is not willing to give up too soon. Loritts highlights that spirit when he observes, "Reliable leaders in the multi-ethnic church are guided by the economics of the kingdom and not the economics of this world."[128] There are a lot of reasons why ministries, especially across lines of difference, do not last.

Why Do Some Ministries Not Make It?

The first of these is that those engaged in this kind of ministry have unrealistic expectations. People enter ministry because they sense that God is calling them to make a difference. This is good and appropriate. There are times, though, when we can interject our own visions of success or meaningful ministry into what is going on. It becomes "our" ministry instead of the work God has called us to do. When "my ministry" does not attain the levels of success or growth that I think it should (or the level others seem to be reaching), then I deem it a failure and am ready to quit. The foolishness of this kind of thinking is clear. Paul writes, "Each one should test their own actions. Then they can take pride in themselves alone, without comparing themselves to someone else" (Gal. 6:4). It is not in our purview to determine what a successful ministry is. The Lord makes that decision. Mother Teresa once said, "God has not called us to be successful, but to be faithful."[129]

The second obstacle for some is the lack of immediate results or impact. There are times when those engaged in ministry, especially ministry across lines of difference, get frustrated and burned out because they do not see immediate results in the work they are doing. Ministry in general, and especially across lines of difference, requires time and patience. Rarely do the ministry results happen on our own timelines. Paul writes, "Let us not become weary in doing good, for at the proper time we will reap a harvest if we do not give up" (Gal. 6:9).

I am reminded of my first-grade class and our project planting seeds and measuring their growth. Like a lot of school projects, we took an empty milk carton from lunch, filled the bottom of it with potting soil, and planted the seeds of our choosing. Some of my classmates chose bean plants of various types. Those were the wise students. They had measurable growth quickly. It was awesome, for a first grader. I, however, was not one of the sharp, young farmers. I planted carrot seeds. I believe nothing could grow more slowly than carrots in a milk carton. While others were measuring and chattering about thin stalks of green spilling over the sides of their milk cartons, I stared at an empty square of dirt. There were quite a few days that I wanted to dig up those seeds just to see what was wrong with them. Why were they not growing? I did not do that, but I thought about it. Finally, after what seemed like forever, tiny little strands of green began to break through the potting soil in my milk carton. I had to wait a long time, but it was worth it.

Who is My Neighbor?

Waiting on the Lord is not easy. Those in ministry are anxious to see results. Like I did in the first grade, they want to know that what they do matters. They want to know that it is alive and growing. I wonder how many times ministry is growing and taking root just beneath the soil, ready to burst forth, only to be dug up and ripped out by an impatient young farmer. Have patience. Don't be in such a hurry.

A third reason some ministries across lines of difference do not continue is that preparation to conduct that kind of ministry does not engage the culture of those to whom and with whom ministry is conducted. There are times when ministry leaders are not culturally prepared to minister to different groups.

Williams, in his book, notes an important truth: "Whether you are called to share the gospel outside the ragged front door of a crack house in the 'hood or with a new neighbor who just moved to town from another state, you are going to have to take some drastic steps to fit into their world."[130] To minister effectively across lines of difference, the minister needs to take time to learn about the world in which he is entering. The people being ministered to are the same at the core level, but their life experiences have shaped them differently. The minister who wants sustainable, successful ministry across lines of difference recognizes this truth.

Williams writes about a Caucasian pastor who was convinced that God had sent him to minister to the black and Latino communities. Williams spoke to him and offered him some friendly advice, books to read, and the experience of life lived in this neighborhood. The minister was polite but did not listen. He began the church and illustrated his sermons with stories of skiing and the mountains. He spoke about redaction criticism and transubstantiation. The church started with a flurry of excitement only to find the seats virtually empty two months later. The church closed and the minister left town and was not heard from again.[131] When ministers are not well-prepared to minister to those from different backgrounds and life experiences, the result is often the same.

A fourth reason some ministries across lines of difference do not make it, is that the life circumstance becomes too hard or uncomfortable. Mark R. Gornik posits, "Staying in the city is about being continually aware of and alert to what God is doing in our midst, to having our assumptions turned upside down and our questions changed, and to the possibility of the unexpected. It is about realizing how little we understand and know about the complexity of our city and life, but even more so, growing from this realization into a deeper, more profound trust in God."[132] Doing ministry in a different environment and context can be difficult. That kind of ministry deals with the unexpected. Those involved in this kind of ministry do not necessarily find the path to be smooth or easy. However, for those who are willing to endure the season of being uncomfortable, the outcome can be incredible. Gornik writes, "We don't know what God will do, what we will see afresh or encounter. But God has invited all of us to stay in the city, to wait to receive power from on high, the gift of the Spirit, and to trust how God is already at work." [133]

Practical Strategies to Facilitate Sustainability

There are some strategies that can assist ministries to sustain. Manny and Blanca Ortiz with Sue and Randy Baker, were able to develop a ministry in Philadelphia that continues to make a difference. They started the ministry in 1987 and have continued it through today. Over that period, they developed leaders and helped start nine neighborhood churches. They also started a Christian school in the neighborhood. They stayed in the city, keeping their commitments and developing lasting relationships.[134] What can a minister do to increase his/her sustainability in a particular ministry?

Prioritize Well

One of the key things to keep in mind regarding ministry across lines of difference is to begin with that which is right in front of you. That is your priority. Simply put, do what you can with the situation as it is. Perhaps that means you have an open dinner for the residents of the neighborhood. Maybe it is simply inviting a couple over for a meal. Maybe it is organizing a school supply drive for the kids in the neighborhood. Do what needs to be done right in front of you.

Who is My Neighbor?

Sometimes ministers can get caught up in what looks flashy or big. They think they have to have a "grand opening." They remind me of Mark Twain's character Tom Sawyer in the book *The Adventures of Huckleberry Finn*. Tom is the same age as Huck and his best friend. Tom was raised in white middle-class comfort. As a result, his belief system is a combination of what he has learned from the adults around him and the ideals he has gleaned from reading adventure stories. He won't do anything unless it is done properly, including rescuing Jim. A blind devotion to doing things the "proper" way can make things difficult. Don't get caught up in that. Do what is evident around you.

Build Relationships

One of the most important things a minister can do in ministering across lines of difference is build relationships with the people they want to serve. This is not a new idea. Cross-cultural missions have been teaching this idea for a long time. Most people understand the need for that in a foreign country. The same is true when ministering to different groups within the United States. Gornik writes, "The heart of ministry is not solving a large societal problem or launching a new church, however significant those are, but being attentive to and valuing relationships."[135]

While ministering in Kansas City, Kansas, I had the opportunity to serve in an area nursing home. Nursing home ministry is important, and I was happy to do it. One of the results of that ministry was that I got to know a number of workers and residents at that facility. I especially remember meeting an African American single mother. I had the chance to encourage her and pray for her and her son. When they wanted to find a church home, they came to the church where I ministered. I had the honor of baptizing her son. All of those things grew out of a relationship that started in a ministry setting. Relationships are important and should not be neglected.

Have a Support System

Ministry is hard. Those who have been in ministry know that. Ministering to those across lines of difference can be really tough.

No one can do it alone. Those who have sustained ministry do so because they have a strong support system. This support system has both a vertical and a horizontal component. The vertical part of the support system is built on a growing, vibrant relationship with Jesus Christ. The minister who neglects his own soul will soon find himself struggling. The minister has to be in the Word regularly. Even as he pours himself out for others, he must be getting "filled up." Prayer is crucial for sustaining a ministry. Elisabeth Eliot said, "Prayer lays hold of God's plan and becomes the link between his will and its accomplishment on earth. Amazing things happen, and we are given the privilege of being the channels of the Holy Spirit's prayer." One who leads others to worship must be a worshiper also. These things cannot be neglected.

The horizontal component of the support system is a circle of supporters, prayer warriors, and family who continue to pray for, encourage, and sponsor the ministry being done. Too many times, ministers go off to do ministry in a "Lone Ranger" fashion. It is easy to become disappointed and discouraged. If there aren't others around to lift up a discouraged minister, it is easy to admit defeat. Solomon wrote, "Though one may be overpowered, two can defend themselves. A cord of three strands is not quickly broken" (Eccl 4:12). People need each other, especially in ministry. A support system can do a lot to strengthen a ministry when things are tough.

Sustainability Involves Recruiting and Training Leaders Well

In addition to strategies mentioned earlier, another key component of a sustainable ministry is training others to lead and engage in the ministry. The roots of this are found in the Bible. Paul challenged Timothy to entrust to others the things he heard Paul teach. The goal is to teach those who will teach others (2 Tim 2:2). The local church can and needs to be the agent for personal life change and community transformation. This is a crucial part of ministry across lines of difference and is vital for ministry sustainability. One of the key components that should be emphasized in this kind of ministry is the "train-the-trainer model."[136] This approach to ministry involves selecting and training people *from the community* to lead the particular community. The church has a unique opportunity to attract people from distinct cultures and backgrounds and can utilize that opportunity to equip them.[137] The indigenous leader must be trained well. This is crucial with respect to authenticity and sustainability. Training must respect the practices and customs of the culture while establishing the foundation of the gospel.[138] This approach will not only develop leaders from within the group but will lead to authentic faith. Recognition of the common humanity shared by different people groups is a foundational principle of spiritual formation and growth.[139] Bringing up leaders from within the group will facilitate long-term ministry effectiveness and develop an environment of sustainability. To do that, there has to be a recognition of a couple of key facts.

See People as People

Efrem Smith notes the greatest need for impoverished neighborhoods is healthy churches.[140] Sustainable ministries in these areas can be difficult. Smith notes his own experience with this phenomenon. In his experience, a person goes into the hood to do good works. Time passes and they become frustrated because people don't "act right." By that they mean they don't uphold upper-middle-class standards. This leads to bitterness, resentment, and the end of the ministry. In Smith's view, residents of the neighborhood are not viewed as people, but as objects that should respond in predetermined ways.[141]

Relationships are built upon trust, respect, and caring. All of these are dependent on seeing others as people with different life experiences and points of reference. The goal is to build enough good will to form healthy relationships, which can lead to sharing the gospel and ultimately discipleship.

Connect Where the People Are

Smith also notes the importance of connecting with the people of the neighborhood where they are, and the areas about which they are most concerned. There are three areas that must be impacted by ministry across lines of difference if it is to be lasting. These areas are family, education, and employment.

Long-lasting ministry across lines of difference will support the family structure of those in the neighborhood. The family structure may not be the traditional model. There will be many single parents who are trying to do it all. If ministry is to take root in these areas, it has to find a place in this soil. How does this ministry support the family structure that is present? It may be that it includes an after-school program. It may need to offer tutoring for students who need assistance. It may need to provide school supplies for families who have limited budgets. It may need to offer babysitting or mothers' groups. These are just a few examples of the ways a ministry can positively impact the family.

The second institution the ministry will need to work with is the neighborhood school. The kids of the neighborhood will all be connected with the school. The parents of the kids will also be involved, to some degree, with the school. Those involved in ministry across lines of difference can make connections with people if they are willing to volunteer in a classroom or substitute teach in their neighborhood school. Being known as a person of the community outside the church building is critical to gaining the respect and credibility needed to succeed.

The final area in which ministry across lines of difference must make a difference is in the job scene. Successful, sustainable ministries help the people find and maintain employment. This is sometimes accomplished by hosting job fairs in the community. It is also important to have training workshops about how to interview for a job and how to fill out an application. Ministries that address these needs demonstrate that they care about the people and want to connect with them.

Summing Up

Sustainability in all kinds of ministry matters, but it is especially important in ministry across lines of differences. Some Christians today are ambivalent about ministering to the urban areas of our country. There are some who believe cities are a negative force that undermine values and faith. The need for sustained, effective ministry in urban areas and across lines of difference is as great now as it has ever been. In *The Encyclopedia of the Stone-Campbell Movement*, Douglas Foster asserts, "Of the three streams of the Stone-Campbell Movement, Christian Churches/Churches of Christ have proportionately the smallest number of African American congregants and members. But in all three branches of the Movement, the journey to harmonious race relations has just begun."[142]

Christians cannot be indifferent to the ever-changing culture of our day. We cannot impact the lost world if we are not engaged with it. To engage, we have to be in ministry with our culture. If a minister cares about having an influence, they will earn that through showing up, caring, and living with those to whom they minister.

Foundational Principles

Chapter 7

Theological Foundation

While it is not often thought of, the foundation of a house or building is important. When foundations fail, the consequences can range from cracks and tilting to the complete collapse of the building or house. Foundation failure jeopardizes the safety of a house or building and those in it. Foundation failure can lead to costly repairs, loss of property, and even loss of life. *The Structured Foundations Blog* lists several examples of structural failure including the Leaning Tower of Pisa, the Quebec Bridge, and the 31-story Ocean Tower on South Padre Island in Texas.[143] Foundations matter. They matter for physical buildings, and they matter in ministry, too. Ministry across lines of difference must be built on a strong, solid theological foundation if it is to be successful and make a difference in the lives of the people it wants to serve.

The theological foundation of ministering across lines of difference is built upon five important theological pillars. The first of those is the nature of the Bible itself. The inerrancy of Scripture is a key component because the challenge to reach others, and the methods utilized to do it are directed by the Word of God. The second pillar is God's desire for all people to repent and come to Him. This is the impetus for ministry of any kind. The third pillar is the nature or universality of sin and its solution. Recognizing that all human beings are sinners and need redemption is crucial for this kind of ministry. The remedy for what is ailing humanity is turning from sin and turning to Jesus Christ. The fourth pillar is God's intention for a multi-ethnic kingdom. The Bible is clear that people of every language, nation, and tribe will come together to worship the Lord. The final pillar is the challenge to teach and disciple those who do not know Jesus. This is the Great Commission (Matt 28:19-20). Teaching others and making disciples is the call of every follower of Jesus and is the objective of ministering across lines of racial, cultural, and socio-economic difference.

Who is My Neighbor?

The Inerrancy of the Bible

The standard by which right and wrong are measured is rooted in the Bible. Inerrancy of Scripture ensures that the standard is trustworthy and reliable. Inerrancy is the acknowledgment that the Scriptures, in their original manuscripts, are without error. The Bible speaks the truth regarding every issue it addresses. Norman Geisler describes inerrancy from the point of view of the framers of the Evangelical Theological Society as he writes, "It comes down to these three principles. (1) God cannot err. (2) The Bible is the Word of God. (3) Therefore, the Bible cannot err. Hence, to deny the inerrancy of the Bible, one must deny either premise 1 or 2 or both."[144] Geisler asserts that the early church fathers held to both classical theism (that God is infinite, unchangeable, and omniscient), and to inerrancy.[145]

Inerrancy has its roots in Scripture. Paul writes, "All Scripture is God-breathed and is useful for teaching, rebuking, correcting and training in righteousness, so that the servant of God may be thoroughly equipped for every good work" (2 Tim 3:16-17). The first significant word or phrase in this text is "All Scripture." In this text, it is important to note that "All Scripture" refers to the Old Testament scriptures which were able to make Timothy wise in preparation for salvation."[146] The next phrase in the verse is critical. "God-breathed" is the word "*theopneustos*" which is used only in this text. Literally, the word means "God breathed."[147] The Scriptures are the product of God's direct interaction with the human authors who penned the words. As he breathed into Adam the breath of life (Gen 2:7), God breathed His message into the hearts and minds of those who penned the Scriptures.

Peter also writes about the nature of Scripture: "Above all, you must understand that no prophecy of Scripture came about by the prophet's own interpretation of things. For prophecy never had its origin in the human will, but prophets, though human, spoke from God as they were carried along by the Holy Spirit" (2 Pet 1:20-21). The key phrase in this passage is "prophets, though human, spoke from God as they were carried along by the Holy Spirit." Edwin A. Blum observes that this implies the dual authorship of Scripture. It is the means by which Scripture was produced.[148] Peter is addressing the reality that God chose to work through human authors to transmit His eternal message. The words of Scripture are, by definition, the words of God. The Bible itself and early church history advocate for inerrancy of Scripture.

There have been challenges to that position. Historically, Deism accepts the reality of God but denies a written revelation from Him. Geisler further explains: "Because of their common denial of miracles, they (Deists) came to the conclusion (logically drawn from their view of God) that the Bible is neither divinely authoritative nor inerrant."[149] Contemporary writers also challenge the concept of inerrancy. Adam Hamilton asserts, "Many mainline Christians and an increasing number of moderate evangelicals have rejected the idea of inerrancy (and verbal, plenary inspiration) that has been championed by conservative Christians, offering instead a view of scripture that takes seriously both the Bible's inspiration from God and the humanity of its biblical authors."[150] Hamilton contends that the Bible does not claim inerrancy for itself, and that the Bible has "errors" and "inconsistencies."[151]

While Hamilton's view and that of the Deists have swayed some, the case for inerrancy remains strong. To insist the Bible does not claim inerrancy for itself is not convincing. The word for "God-breathed" means literally, "God-breathed," not "God-inspired" as Hamilton asserts.[152] Hamilton posits that there are conflicting stories in the gospels that simply cannot be reconciled. He cites the women who visit the tomb on the first day of the week. He notes the differences in each gospel account, concludes that they cannot be harmonized, and decides the Bible is in error. In his view, all resurrection accounts should be viewed as simply acknowledging Jesus' resurrection.[153] However, the texts can be harmonized, and inerrancy of Scripture preserved.[154] It is not the focus of this book to explain that harmony in detail, but a quick summary reveals that the women came from Bethany, which was about two miles away. It was likely that they left before the sun rose and arrived very early in the morning. At least five women went, though not all are named. Two angels appear to them. All of them rush back to the other disciples in Bethany except Mary Magdalene who goes to Jerusalem where Peter and John were. There are many more details, but the inerrancy of Scripture is not lost by apparent contradictions.

Inerrancy of Scripture is important for ministry across lines of difference. The basis for right and wrong is rooted in the fact that the Bible is God's Word. As such, it defines what is pleasing to God and what is not. It conveys God's commands to His people and His desires for them. Ministry in general and especially across lines of difference intends to motivate people to actions that are explicitly biblical. This kind of ministry, built upon the truth of the Bible, calls people to live out the commands of Scripture. Confidence that the Bible reflects God's view of the world accurately is crucial for this kind of ministry to succeed.

God's Desire for All People to Repent

The second theological pillar on which this kind of ministry stands is God's desire for all people to repent and return to Him. Paul urged that petitions, prayers, intercession, and thanksgiving be made for all people— for kings and those in authority. The reason is so Christians may live peaceful and quiet lives in all godliness and holiness, for this is good and pleases God. The next phrase in the verse is critical. God "wants all people to be saved and to come to a knowledge of the truth. For there is one God and one mediator between God and mankind, the man Christ Jesus, who gave himself as a ransom for all people" (1 Tim 2:1-6). Ralph Earle writes of this passage, "Salvation has been provided for all, but only those who accept it are saved."[155] God's desire is for all people to come to Him through the sacrifice of Jesus Christ. Philip H. Towner observes, "The theme of the passage is salvation, and 'savior' depicts God as the source and architect of the plan to rescue humanity through Christ."[156] It is evident that God wants a relationship with all humanity and developed the plan by which fallen humanity could be restored and redeemed. That plan is rooted deeply in the nature, person, and work of His son Jesus Christ.

God's desire for all people to know about Jesus and accept Him as Savior and Lord is also seen in John 3. God has offered salvation through Jesus to the whole world. He does not want to condemn the world, but to save the world through Him (John 3:16-17). Frederick Dale Bruner writes of these verses, "The wonderfully divine way into the Spirit's transformation is simple trust in the divine human Son given for and to us needy creatures in the whole wide world."[157] Those in the "whole wide world" can experience transformation by trusting in the Son of God, Jesus Christ. Craig S. Keener writes of this verse, "In Johannine theology God's love for the 'world' represents his love for all humanity."[158] Colin Cruse concurs, "It was God's love for all humanity that led him to give his one and only Son."[159] John 3:16 indicates that God loved all humanity and sent Jesus to die so that all might have eternal life.

The nature of God's kingdom indicates His desire for all people to have a relationship with Him. The Great Commission (Matt 28:19-20), in which disciples are to be made of "all nations" (*panta ta ethne*), addresses this issue. Daniel Doriani writes of this passage, "A universal mission has been in view since Genesis 12, and Matthew often points to a Gentile mission."[160] From the beginning, God has intended for the message of salvation to reach all people. This point is also seen in the book of Revelation. Revelation 5:9-10 describes the song of the twenty-four elders. In that song, they proclaim, "with your blood you purchased for God persons from every tribe and language and people and nation." Gordon Fee writes of this passage, "John is affirming one of the frequent themes in the eschatological outlook of the Prophets— as well as the major passion in the ministry of Paul—that God chose Israel so that through them he might bless the whole world."[161]

God's desire is for all people to repent and come to Him. This is a foundational principle for success in this kind of ministry. Ministry across lines of cultural, racial, and socio-economic differences happens because God loves the world. It is evident from Scripture that God's intent has been to reach all people with the good news of Jesus Christ. God's desire for a kingdom of all people becomes the motivation for this kind of ministry.

Who is My Neighbor?

The Universality of Sin and Its Solution

The third pillar on which this ministry stands is the universality of sin and its solution. All human beings are sinners and need repentance, restoration, and salvation. Paul writes, "For everyone has sinned; we all fall short of God's glorious standard" (Rom 3:23). Everett F. Harrison concurred, "The reason all must come to God through faith in Christ is that all have sinned and fall short of the glory of God."[162] Every human being is a sinner. This is an important truth for ministry across lines of difference. Recognition of the sin nature is crucial. Prejudice, racism, hatred, jealousy, greed, legalism, and a plethora of other acts that displease God come from the same root. Human beings are sinners. It is only through the recognition of this that repentance and restoration can happen.

This is not a new idea. Solomon wrote, "Indeed, there is no one on earth who is righteous, no one who does what is right and never sins" (Eccl 7:20). J. Stafford Wright observes about this passage, "There is no such thing as sinless perfection."[163] No human being can live up to the standard of perfection. Sin corrodes the lives of every human being and is the reason for the separation from the Creator. Sin is humanity's greatest problem.

The solution is not found in human action. It is only through God's grace and the sacrifice of Jesus that the sin problem is resolved. Only the blood of Jesus Christ can atone for sin (Heb 9:22 and Rom 6:23). Jesus acknowledged this while sharing the Passover meal with His disciples just hours before the crucifixion. Jesus took a cup and said, "Drink from it, all of you. This is my blood of the covenant, which is poured out for many for the forgiveness of sins" (Matthew 26:27-28). D. A. Carson observes that this text indicates that Jesus knew that his violent death would ratify the covenant he was inaugurating with his people: "The event through which Messiah saves his people from their sins is his sacrificial death."[164] Paul acknowledges this in his farewell to the Ephesian elders. He challenges them to, "Be shepherds of the church of God, which he bought with his own blood" (Acts 20:28).

Having established that the shed blood of Jesus is the basis for salvation, the Christian's response is repentance and baptism. When asked what to do, Peter told the crowd on the Day of Pentecost, "Repent and be baptized, every one of you, in the name of Jesus Christ for the forgiveness of your sins. And you will receive the gift of the Holy Spirit" (Acts 2:38). John notes, "If we confess our sins, he is faithful and just and will forgive us our sins and purify us from all unrighteousness" (1 John 1:9). Of the Acts passage, Darrell L. Bock writes, "Peter is telling his audience to change direction from the attitudes that led them to crucify Jesus and look to God through Jesus for forgiveness."[165] This is the picture of repentance. John Painter writes of John's epistle, "The consequence of such confession is that God is faithful and righteous to forgive sins and to cleanse from unrighteousness."[166]

Repentance leads to a restored relationship with God. Forgiveness is offered and God and sinner are reconciled. Paul writes, "For if, while we were God's enemies, we were reconciled to him through the death of his Son, how much more, having been reconciled, shall we be saved through his life" (Rom 5:10). The Greek word for reconciled is from the root word "*katallasso*," which notes an exchange or change. In this context, the exchange is one from enemy to friendship.[167] Reconciliation is the result of the process of dealing with the sin issue. Reconciliation with God and then with others is a major characteristic of successful ministry across lines of difference.

A Multi-Ethnic Kingdom

The fourth theological pillar on which ministry across lines of difference rests is God's desire for a multi-ethnic kingdom. In his address at the Areopagus, Paul declared to the Athenians, and all gathered there that God made all nations from one man. His purpose was that they should inhabit the earth. He even appointed the times they would reign and the boundaries of their lands. All of this was for one purpose, "God did this so that they would seek him and perhaps reach out for him and find him, though he is not far from any one of us" (Acts 17:27). Of this verse, C.K. Barrett asserts that human beings "were made with a view to their seeking God."[168] God's intention, from the beginning, was for a kingdom of all people.

Who is My Neighbor?

The result of that desire is seen in John's vision as recorded in the book of Revelation. "After this I looked, and there before me was a great multitude that no one could count, from every nation, tribe, people, and language, standing before the throne and before the Lamb. They were wearing white robes and were holding palm branches in their hands" (Rev 7:9). Alan F. Johnson notes that these were people from every cultural background, both Jews and Gentiles.[169] The kingdom of God reflects diversity.

The early church struggled with the issue of diversity. The Jerusalem council wrestled with the question of whether Gentile Christians had to be circumcised. Paul and Barnabas disagreed with those who advocated for Gentile circumcision. As Acts 15 notes, the apostles and elders met to resolve this issue. After describing his own realization that Gentiles were part of God's plan, Peter declared, "He did not discriminate between us and them, for he purified their hearts by faith" (Acts 15:9). Longenecker asserts that Peter is aligning himself with Paul and insisting that God had already indicated his approval of a Gentile outreach that did not require circumcision.[170] John T. Squires observes that Peter concludes by urging acceptance of what Paul and Barnabas have done, since those Jews who believe have received salvation in the same way as Gentile believers did, through the grace of the Lord Jesus. He adds, "In this way, he argues that the God who is not partial has clearly been at work both in events in Caesarea, which Peter experienced, and in the activity of Paul and Barnabas throughout Asia Minor. The assemblies they established are inclusive—Gentiles belong just as much as Jews."[171] The message of the Jerusalem council is that God desires all people, Jew, and Gentile, to be citizens of His kingdom.

The church, early in her history, struggled with the identity and nature of Christians. The determination of the Jerusalem council was clear. God's kingdom was larger than the covenant requirements of the Jews. His kingdom was for all people. For successful ministry across lines of difference, this is one of the central principles. As the early church struggled with the multi-ethnic nature of the kingdom, the church today struggles. The need for ministry across lines of difference has never been more urgent. Doing this kind of ministry fulfills God's intention for the nature of His kingdom.

A Challenge to Teach and Disciple

The final theological pillar on which this kind of ministry rests is the challenge to teach and disciple others. Jesus said as He ascended into heaven, "Therefore go and make disciples of all nations, baptizing them in the name of the Father and of the Son and of the Holy Spirit, and teaching them to obey everything I have commanded you. And surely, I am with you always, to the very end of the age" (Matt 28:19-20). This is at the heart of ministry across lines of difference because it is at the heart of all ministry. Carson writes of this verse, "To disciple a person to Christ is to bring him into the relation of pupil to teacher." He adds, "Disciples are those who hear, understand, and obey Jesus' teaching."[172] The imperative in Jesus' words, before He ascended, was to "make disciples." Christians must reach out to others to share with them the good news.

Luke records Jesus' final words to the disciples before returning to heaven. Jesus said, "But you will receive power when the Holy Spirit comes on you; and you will be my witnesses in Jerusalem, and in all Judea and Samaria, and to the ends of the earth" (Acts 1:8). This was the marching order that Jesus gave his disciples before ascending into heaven. The order Jesus gives encompasses the world. The message of the gospel is for every people group across the world. Richard Longenecker writes of this verse, "This commission lays an obligation on all Christians and comes to us as a gift with a promise." He continues, "The Christian church, according to Acts, is a missionary church that responds obediently to Jesus' commission, acts on Jesus' behalf in the extension of his ministry and focuses on the proclamation of the kingdom of God in its witness to Jesus."[173] Longenecker highlights the responsibility that followers of Jesus must take the gospel to those who do not know Him or have a relationship with Him.

The Bible is clear about the mandate Christians have to make disciples of all people. When Jesus saw the crowds of people, Matthew notes He had compassion on them because they were harassed and helpless, like sheep without a shepherd. So, he said to his disciples, "The harvest is plentiful, but the workers are few. Ask the Lord of the harvest, therefore, to send out workers into his harvest field" (Matt 9:37-38). The harvest is still plentiful today. There are people across this nation and around the globe who need to hear about Jesus. This must be the essence of ministry across lines of difference.

For ministry across lines of difference, this pillar is critical. Taking the good news of Jesus to people of different cultural, racial, and socio-economic backgrounds is at the heart of ministry and diversity. Ernest Easley writes of the command to make disciples, "That is a mandate to the church and therefore should be a priority in our lives."[174] That mandate must be emphasized in preparing to minister to a wide variety of people.

Summing Up

A solid foundation matters for builders of homes and hearts. The theological foundation upon which effective ministry across lines of difference rests is important. To be successful, this kind of ministry is grounded in the truth and authority of the Word of God. It is driven by a desire to see all people enter a saving relationship with Jesus Christ. It understands the root of humanity's problem is sin. It champions that God's kingdom is big and broad, encompassing people of every tribe, nation, and tongue. Finally, it is demonstrated in the reality of teaching and baptizing disciples of Jesus. Ministry that is built on this kind of foundation can be effective, strong, and meaningful.

Chapter 8

Theoretical Foundations

The Three Little Pigs is a fairy tale that most people have heard or read. The story traces its roots back to a book called *English Fairy Tales* written by Joseph Jacobs in 1890. The story is familiar and simple. There are three little pigs, brothers, who build houses in the woods. One builds his house with straw, the second of sticks, and the third builds his house out of bricks. Most preschool children realize the difference in the building materials used by the pigs, so they are not surprised when the Big Bad Wolf comes to visit each pig. He first visits the pig in the house of straw. He huffs and puffs and easily blows down that house. The little pig runs as fast as he can to his brother in the straw house. However, that house suffers the same fate, and the pigs scamper to the brother who lives in the brick house. The wolf comes to that house, too, but is unable to blow that house down.

Only the brick house can stand up to the huffing and puffing of the Big Bad Wolf. Straw and sticks are not practical building materials. The pigs who used them were lazy and careless. The house of the practical pig was the only one to survive. Practicality matters in fairy tales. It also matters in ministry across lines of difference.

Not only must ministering across lines of difference be built on a strong theological foundation, but it should also have a solid foundation of practical concepts and actions. This kind of ministry is often part of a larger urban ministry outreach. Roger Gench contends that urban areas wrestle with a wide range of predicaments that require ministries to display a willingness to make a difference and the humility to know how to do that in an effective manner.[175] Ministry students need to be equipped and trained to deal with those issues. In addition to the solid theological foundation upon which this ministry needs to be built, there are three theoretical, practical truths upon which this kind of ministry is built. Those truths are presence, humility, and engagement. These three practices support ministry of this kind and provide it with a foundation from which meaning and impact can come.

Presence

The first of these practical truths is presence. Harvie M. Conn and Manuel Ortiz surmise that future historians will record the twentieth century as a time in which the entire world became a huge city.[176] More people live in urban areas than at any other time in history.[177] The population of cities is incredibly diverse as people from different cultures, backgrounds, and races live together.[178] There has never been a time better than now for effective ministry to these diverse people groups. Presence is the commitment to be there, stay there, and make a difference there, which is crucial for success in this kind of ministry.

Effective ministry to people of different backgrounds begins with presence or a desire to be there. Williams asserts that presence in the neighborhood is crucial to ministering to those who live there. People who live in the cities are "looking for believers who aren't afraid to greet them on the avenue and ask how they are doing and mean it."[179] The importance of being there and willing to interact cannot be overstated. Its impact can be felt throughout the community. Regarding city life, Gornik and Wong explain, "Whether in a small city or large global city, in a changing neighborhood where new restaurants and businesses are arriving, in a community where lives are always in precarious balance, or in a place of prime real estate and executive offices, the vocation of urban Christians begins with presence."[180]

There is an old adage in the church that says, "The most important ability you need in doing ministry in the church is your availability." For ministry to be successful, people can't phone it in. Presence makes a difference. Being there for the people to whom you are ministering may be the single most important thing.

Patricia Fordney of Corvallis, Oregon, understands this truth. She describes a time when her husband, who was in the Navy, was on extended duty overseas. She was having a tough time balancing her full-time job and caring for their toddler. One evening, the doorbell rang. It was her neighbor, a retired Naval officer, carrying a breadboard loaded with freshly grilled chicken and vegetable stew. It was a moment she never forgot. A caring neighbor simply showed up to make a difference.[181]

Michelle Arnold knows the importance of people being there. She writes about the time when she lived in California and got lost on the wrong freeway. She had no idea where she should go. She called her roadside-assistance provider who tried to connect her to the California Highway Patrol, but the call could not get through. The woman on the line with Michelle heard the panic in her voice and came up with another idea. She told Michelle that she wasn't far from her. She told her she would come to her and lead her back to the right freeway. Ten minutes later, the woman drove up and led Michelle to the right exit. An emergency worker was willing to go the extra mile to just be there for a lost motorist.[182]

Shelly Golay of Casper, Wyoming, gives a final testimony to the importance of showing up and just doing the little things. She writes about her neighbors, Jay and Treva, whom she and her husband first met when they moved to the neighborhood. Shelly's husband got brain cancer, which brought them great stress. Jay and Treva proved to be more than neighborly as they shoveled snow, provided meals, and did whatever yard and maintenance work was needed. When her husband passed away, Shelly wrote of how Jay and Treva continued to reach out, even in something as simple as putting away the trash can. Shelly concluded her story by noting that no matter what she needed, she could count on Jay and Treva to be there for her.[183] Showing up, even in the simplest of ways, makes a difference.

Successful ministries with those of different backgrounds and in urban areas are built on the foundation of presence. Consistently being there does more than people realize. The interactions that occur and the relationships that are formed become fuel for lasting, meaningful ministry.

Humility

The second crucial component of the theoretical foundation is humility. Humility is a practical but sometimes rare trait that needs to inundate all that a minister does. Ministry with people of different races, backgrounds, and cultures is only effective if it comes from a humble, authentic heart. Williams describes that kind of heart. It begins with the willingness to take drastic steps to fit into the culture of the people being reached, and a desire to understand their backgrounds.[184]

Fans of the television show *Lost in Space* might remember the Robinson family and their travels through the universe with meddling Dr. Smith and the Robot. From the Cyclops to the Golden Man, Keema, they encountered all kinds of different life forms and cultures. They had to figure out how to communicate, interact with, and ultimately respect each of them. Williams asserts that those who minister across lines of difference, especially in urban areas, face the same challenge. The person being ministered to may share the same skin color and hair texture, but their view of life has been shaped by a different reality.[185] Understanding and respecting that truth is vital if ministry is to be sustained and successful.

The next step is not assuming that there is one correct way to worship, praise, or encounter the Lord Jesus Christ.[186] This is a critical aspect of successful ministry across lines of diversity. Unfortunately, many ministries to different people have been short-lived because the minister could only see one way to do things.[187] Loritts asserts that white evangelicals' inability to see things from a different perspective hinders true Christian unity and fellowship within the body of Christ.[188] The way the predominantly white culture practices evangelical faith has often become the default setting for all of evangelical worship. Loritts says it this way, "Since the first European immigrants set foot in America in the 1600s, Christianity has been played in the stadium of what we now know as white evangelicalism. White evangelicalism has been the home team. Look hard enough, and many African American Christians can trace their spiritual lineage back to whites in this country. And because theology always comes with its unique ethnic accent, most of what has been handed to us is a theology done in white."[189] It isn't hard to understand how that happens. For those who want to successfully minister across lines of difference, an intentional effort to experience other things is necessary.

While ministering in Kansas City, I remember meeting an African American pastor at a nearby church, and he and I worked together on a community project that was successful. As a result, we developed a friendship. We decided it would be good to exchange pulpits and preach in each other's churches. Though I had been to an African American church before, I had never preached at one. I still remember the amazing experience of preaching at my friend's church. The energy and passion of the congregation and the joy of the music were expressed in ways I had not experienced previously. It was different than where I came from, but it was genuine and powerful. I know from my conversations with my friend, he noticed differences in the way we worshiped. It was clear that neither style of worship was better than the other. They were different expressions of adoration and praise. I worshiped as honestly in my friend's church as I did each week in my own church. Though different ethnic groups or cultures express praise and worship differently, if it is directed to the Lord and genuine, all of it is pleasing to him. It is the fulfillment of what Jesus wants his people to do. Paul writes, "Be completely humble and gentle; be patient, bearing with one another in love" (Eph 4:2). Ministry across lines of difference must be built on this important truth. Humility requires that one sees value and worth in doing something differently than what one would normally do.

Baseball fans will recall the name Miguel Cabrera. Cabrera is a future Hall of Fame player who won two Most Valuable Player awards and was the first player since 1967 to win baseball's Triple Crown (leader in batting average, home runs, and runs batted in). Cabrera began his career with the Florida Marlins and was there for five years. He then spent the rest of his career playing for the Detroit Tigers. Most baseball fans know Cabrera as an amazing hitter. What is often forgotten is that Cabrera was a versatile fielder. In 2016, he was one of forty major league players to have played over seven hundred games at multiple defensive positions. His view of baseball and perhaps of life can be summed up by one of his well-known statements, "Don't be afraid to give up the good to go for the great." That statement packs more of a wallop than a Cabrera home run. What is true in professional sports is also true in ministry. Locking in to only one way of seeing or doing something is a recipe for failure. Think creatively. Listen well to what others have done or are doing. Don't be afraid to try new things.

Who is My Neighbor?

Another important result of a humble approach to ministry is the development of relationships. Relationships are cultivated by a gentle, humble, unassuming spirit. Ministering across lines of diversity in a humble way can develop personal relationships that are built on honesty.[190] The culmination of honest, humble relationships is community. That's a word that is used frequently in Christian circles today. Community matters in every form of ministry and establishing a sense of community is crucial for effective ministry across lines of difference. Community can be the context for forgiveness, vulnerability, and trust.[191] What must be emphasized is transparency, humility, and honesty, while working with those of different backgrounds and cultures. This will facilitate relationships that can develop in communities of believers.

Engagement

Larry Canton of Tuscaloosa, Alabama, wrote about the impact that small churches can have on the lives of the people around them. He observes that an online course or sermon can reach thousands of people with a salvation message, it is the face-to-face encounter that usually makes the difference. Canton and twenty other Christians go into the Tuscaloosa County Jail each Tuesday night to teach and preach. The men there get to hear worship songs, preaching, and interact in person with other Christians. To those men, that's a big deal. Canton writes, "We are physically there for the inmates. They know that the love and devotion are real, even if the preaching and teaching may not blow them over one night or another. This is both a small thing, and a big thing. Anyone with a calling to help others in Christian love can do it."[192] Canton's work in the Tuscaloosa County Jail highlights the importance of engagement or simply being involved with those with whom one is ministering.

Engagement is the third and final piece of the theoretical foundation for successful ministry across lines of difference. In the context of ministry, engagement is the desire and ability to interact with culture and demonstrate the nature, person, and work of Jesus Christ.[193] Williams describes engagement vividly: "Jesus didn't go into the hood hollering 'turn or burn!' He healed, he visited the lonely, he danced at weddings, he taught, and he journeyed with folks. He went around doing good. Often that would lead to a dialogue about faith; sometimes it didn't. However, even when he didn't verbalize it, he lived it."[194] "Living it" is an apt description of engagement.

What does "living it" look like? Consider the story of Luke Nelson. In 2018, Luke was in the third grade at Oklahoma Christian School in Edmund, Oklahoma. In November of that year, Luke's hair suddenly started to fall out. He was diagnosed with Alopecia areata, an autoimmune skin disease, causing hair loss on the scalp, face and sometimes on other areas of the body. Luke and his family were devastated. Understandably, Luke did not want to go back to school. That is, until he heard about what some of his friends in the third grade had planned. About a dozen third-grade boys from Luke's class decided that if Luke couldn't have hair on his head, they wouldn't either. Their parents agreed and they all met and had their heads shaved at Edmonds Sports Clips who did the haircuts for free. Luke's mother, Susan, shared on social media, "At just 8 years old these kids have done something for Luke that has been truly life-changing — they showed up when he needed them most," Nelson wrote. "Hair or no hair, no one cares. At the end of the day these kids showed Luke (and all of us!) what it means to be brave, and more importantly to be kind."[195]

Engagement is seen in walking alongside people. Missionaries to foreign countries know this. Walking alongside people as you work, serve, and minister with them is crucial for long-term mission success. A course description in a Bible college catalog states the purpose of the class: "This class helps participants recognize the influence of their own cultural perspective in a cross-cultural setting, discover myriad ways we communicate beyond our spoken words, increase sensitivity to cross-cultural interactions, and become effective communicators in multiple worldview contexts."[196] The principle of becoming effective communicators in a place of different worldviews is a part of this missions class and some others like it. Ministry across lines of difference has a similar objective but is different in that it challenges the minister to consider different worldviews and life experiences *within* the context of a vast American culture. The mission field is not just across the ocean but is sometimes across the river into the city on the eastern part of the state. The mission field is not just in villages but can also be in the hood. The church needs effective communicators in these areas, too. While work in the mission field worldwide is vital and should not be neglected, there is a need to minister across lines of difference in our own neighborhoods. The church and Bible college need to ask the question, "How do we minister effectively to fellow Americans who are not like us?" While the "Judea, Samaria, and the ends of earth" (Acts 1:8) need attention, we cannot afford to neglect "Jerusalem." Engagement is a major part of ministry in any circumstance, but it is especially vital in ministry across lines of difference. May the areas that are close to home remain close to the heart.

Liz McEwan notes the importance of remembering the mission field close to home. She and her husband moved to Cincinnati, Ohio in 2003. Having been there for thirteen years, she writes, "One of the unique callings of Christians today is to model faithfulness in the city. Cities are being populated by a new class of young professionals. But in neighborhoods like ours, there are far more restaurants open for brunch on Sunday mornings than there are churches open for worship. Many of these new urbanites were introduced to the Christian faith as children but are estranged from it." She also notes her strong conviction: "The city is a mission field. I believed that before I moved here, and I believe it still. I would even go so far as to say that, in the United States, it is the most urgent mission field of the twenty-first century, one that Christians absolutely must engage with if they want to see the gospel take root in the next few generations."[197] The fact that this ministry is vital is underscored by the fact that there are twenty major metropolitan areas in the United States where the evangelical population is under 6%.[198] It is also important to note that there are about thirty-nine million people in Los Angeles or New York City who do not know Jesus Christ as their Savior. There are three million in Atlanta, and eight million lost people in Chicago alone.[199] The field is "ripe for harvest" (John 4:35) within the United States. The diversity of people in American cities needs Jesus Christ. The time is now for ministers to engage in this kind of work.

Summing Up

More attention is being given to multi-ethnic churches and ministry in the urban areas of the United States, but there is still work to be done. Timothy Keller asserts, "Many Christians today, especially in the United States, are indifferent or even hostile toward cities."[200] Keller continues, "Sadly, there has never been a city on earth that is not saturated with human sin and corruption. Indeed, to paraphrase a Woody Allen joke, cities are just like everywhere else, only much more so."[201] Because of the difficulties and challenges of the city, many Christians are reluctant to engage in or work with diverse population groups. Where it exists, this is an unfortunate and unacceptable mindset. The opportunity to minister to city populations has never been greater. To do so, there must be a commitment to minister across lines of racial, cultural, and socio-economic differences. That commitment must have a practical way of expressing itself. Presence, humility, and engagement are the practical triplet that empowers successful ministry across lines of difference.

Tough Issues

Chapter 9

Ministry to those of Same Sex Attraction

The family attended the church for more than two decades. Their two children had been a part of the children's ministry and youth group and were active in it. On the surface, it seemed as if everything was going smoothly. Looks, though, can be deceiving. During his sophomore year at the high school, their son, the oldest, started struggling with his identity. He did not have many dates and began wondering whether he was attracted to females. He shared some of those concerns with others at school and soon was meeting after school with a group that affirmed his same-sex attraction. He kept it quiet for about a year, not even his parents or his sister knew. His friends suspected it, but no one said anything. He continued this for almost two years. Near the end of his senior year, he decided it was time. On a Saturday night he met with his parents and told them he was gay. They were stunned, and at a loss for what to do. Before long he would be off to college and on his own. What could they do? What should they do?

This scenario is real. Most of the time people understand it happens, but usually to other people. I have spoken with several different parents whose child has, at some point, made the declaration that they are attracted to the same sex. The parents I've spoken to want to know what to do. I have been involved in a Bible quizzing ministry for over thirty-eight years. In the last decade, one of the most troubling concerns of those in leadership is the number of students who have "come out," announcing that they are gay. Statistics support our anecdotal evidence. Public Religion Research Institute (PRRI) polling and focus groups show that 28% of Gen Z adults (ages 18-25) identify as LGBTQ+, which is substantially higher than what's been reported by other sources.[202] The number of Gen Z students identifying as having same-sex attractions is more than double that of the previous generation.[203] What is the church's response to this phenomenon? What do we tell parents? Can we reach out to those who claim same-sex attraction?

This has become one of the most divisive issues affecting the church. This issue has split churches and families. There are churches that are accommodating and affirming the homosexual lifestyle. However, if a church is to remain faithful to the truth of the Bible, then that is not an option. What do churches and ministries who hold the Bible in high regard do about this issue? If the message of the church is to remain relevant, it must address this growing number of people. To minister effectively, it is important to understand the discussion. There are some important issues that have to be addressed and discussed by those who want to reach out to this group.

Be Aware of Spiritual Needs

One of the first truths one seeking to minister across lines of difference must understand is that there are a lot of people who deal with same-sex attractions that want to have a meaningful, spiritual life. The UCLA Williams Institute reports that almost 5.3 million people that identify as LGBT say that religion is important to them, or they attend church.[204] A Pew Research poll indicates that nearly 75% of people who identify as gay believe the evangelical church is unfriendly to them and that nearly four out of five say the Catholic church is hostile to them.[205] The inevitable conclusion is that most people who identify as homosexual and want to attend church, attend a non-evangelical Protestant church that is willing to accept same-sex attraction as an acceptable choice. While there is a substantial number of people in this group interested in spiritual things, the challenge is greater because there are several churches that accept and promote that lifestyle. Though it is a steep climb, it is important to continue to try to reach this group with the good news of new life in Jesus. Like other fields in our culture, this one is ready for harvest. Recognize it is a group that can be reached.

Keep the Doors Open

One of the biggest obstacles of reaching this group is the perception that Jesus doesn't love them, and the church doesn't want them.

Nothing is further from the truth. The sin of acting on same-sex attraction is no greater sin than gossiping, lying, or overeating. The church must be a place where sinners are welcome. Jesus came for the sick, not the healthy. He came to call sinners to repent (Luke 5:31-32). There is difficulty with this in our culture. Many times, people who act upon same-sex attractions do not consider it a sin. They are not open to it being put in that category. Keeping the doors open doesn't mean we shut down the truth. The church must continue to speak as the Bible directs. However, for those who will hear the truth, regardless of their sin, they should be welcomed.

When I was ministering in a mid-size church in the mid-1990's, a man visited our church. He was a kind man and a talented musician. Some of our congregation had heard him play the keyboard at an event. They invited him to church and hoped he would play. He came to church for a couple of months and seemed to like it. The calls for him to become part of the worship team were growing louder. He sent me a message and asked that I meet him for lunch. I was glad to do so. At lunch, we exchanged a few pleasantries, then he told me how much he liked the church. He loved the people and appreciated the preaching. I was happy to hear that. I was ready to see if he would take on a role in the worship team when he said, "I need to tell you something. I'm gay." The direct approach was not as common in the mid-1990's as it is today. I was surprised by what he said but did not have a noticeable reaction. He then told me how nervous he was to share that with me. He thought I might go "Westboro Baptist" on him and kick him out of the church. I told him he would not be kicked out of the church and he was welcome to come any and every week. I told him that there might be times when he would hear a message about the homosexual lifestyle and how it wasn't what God wanted for his people. I told him we believe the Bible to be God's Word and would teach that, not every message or every week, but it would come up. I told him that if he did not want to live that lifestyle, we would pray for him and do what we could to help. I told him if he lived that lifestyle, he would not be able to be a leader. However, he could always come. He appreciated my reply. In his words, it was not hateful but honest. He did come a few more times but later went to a church that promoted that lifestyle.

Did I handle that situation correctly? I'm not sure. I wanted to hold to the truth of the Bible and keep the doors of the church open to those who might want to come. Ultimately, he did not turn away from that lifestyle but found a place that accepted it. I'm not sure if that approach was successful. It is hard to define success in this area. Holding to the truth while demonstrating love is crucial. That's the balance that we must have in this area. It isn't easy. All people must know that Jesus loves them and we love them. There is no more important message for those who are lost than "Jesus loves you." We have to stand for truth. We have to promote righteousness. We need to do both of these things in the bigger context of love. That's what Jesus did.

This is important, not only in ministry, but in how we talk to families who are dealing with this issue. Keeping the doors open is important within the family. How each family deals with this situation is different. However, it is never wrong to tell people, whether they are living in the way of Jesus or not, that he loves them, and you do too.

Understand the Different Views About Same-Sex Attraction

There are three different views of same-sex attractions in today's culture. The first maintains the position that same-sex attractions are normal and fall within the range of acceptable human behavior. Many medical experts believe sexual orientation is not something that a person voluntarily chooses. Sexual orientation is a natural part of who a person is. There's nothing wrong with being LGBT (Lesbian, Gay, Bi-Sexual or Transgender).[206] This is the point of view most often taught in public schools and is reflected in both the media and culture. This view holds that same-sex attractions, transgenderism, and bi-sexuality are acceptable lifestyle choices.

There is public support for this position. In a May 2, 2022, Gallup Poll, seventy-one percent of Americans polled believed gay and lesbian relationships were morally acceptable.[207] Sixty percent of Americans in May of 2022 believe gender is determined at birth, but almost forty percent believe it may be different than the birth gender.[208] For many in today's culture, this is the prevailing view.

A second view, loosely connected to the first, is also found in society and in some churches. It adds spiritual support to the first approach. This view holds that the Bible does not condemn monogamous, same-sex attractions. Those who hold this view assert that, while the words of Scripture do not change, how verses are interpreted must change over time.[209] This view teaches that the Scriptures that speak against acting on same-sex attractions are being misunderstood by Christians today. For example, those who hold this position often argue that Sodom was destroyed, not because of the sin of homosexual conduct, but the sin of violence, arrogance, aggression, or gang-rape.[210] Those who adhere to this view interpret Scripture through the lens of culture, both at the time of the text and the current culture. There is a tendency among those who hold this position to redefine a "high view of Scripture." The Bible is not inerrant or "God-breathed," but is "God-influenced."[211] This view of the Bible allows for passages that address God's view of same-sex attraction to be reinterpreted or dismissed. This is the position of many progressive churches in the United States and around the world.

The third view is different from the first two. The first two views or some combination of them are more popular in the United States today, but popularity does not define what is right. The question is not what people think, but what is God's view. The key to answering that, lies in the nature of the Bible. For those who do not hold to the inerrancy of Scripture, either of the previous views can be supported. Bible passages that speak against same-sex attraction can be reinterpreted to mean what best fits the narrative. If the Bible is not the final arbiter of what is true, then either of the previous two positions on same-sex attraction can be advanced. However, if the Bible is the inerrant Word of God, then it is much more difficult to hold one of those two positions. Despite attempts to spin the text to mean something else, the words of the Bible are clear on this topic. Both the Old and the New Testaments reveal God's view of this contentious issue (Lev 18:22 and 1 Cor 6:9-10). Regardless of how many churches today seek to redefine God's Word on this debate, the Bible's message is evident. Simply put, the third view notes that acting on these urges is not what God wants for His people. Those who seek to minister across this line must be tethered to this truth. While attempting to reach this group, the truth cannot be compromised.

Difficulty in Ministering to Those of Same-Sex Attraction

For those who hold to the inerrancy of Scripture, ministering to those with same-sex attractions is hard. The message for those who do not know Jesus is simple, "Jesus loves you and died for you." It is important to understand that we will probably not convince, persuade, or argue someone out of being same sex attracted. Only Jesus, through the work of the Holy Spirit, can change or transform a person in that way. Our task is to point them to Jesus and get out of the way. What is the problem? For people to experience the transformation Jesus brings, they have to acknowledge that what they were doing is wrong. Whether it be an addiction, theft, greed, or lust, they have to realize it is wrong and want to change. For many of those who are living out a homosexual lifestyle, there is reluctance to acknowledge that as wrong or sinful. It isn't a sin greater or lesser than other sins, but it is not a lifestyle that honors God. However, if they are interested in spiritual things, they can find multiple churches that affirm a homosexual lifestyle. They don't have to deal with it as a sin because they are told it isn't. That, I believe, makes our challenge even tougher.

Recognizing these difficulties, what does ministry to this diverse culture look like? Taking truth to a culture that resists the truth is challenging. Building on the foundation of the authority of the Bible, the initial response must be one of love and compassion. Christians who hold the Bible to be inerrant cannot accept same-sex attraction as normative. However, it is equally true that Christians are not to judge those outside the church (1 Cor 5:12). Christians are to be sympathetic, compassionate, and Christ-like with those who do not know Jesus (1 Pet 3:8). Humility and love must lead in discussions about same-sex attractions. The task of the minister is not to change sinners but to bring them to Jesus. Christians have been called to love and engage people in the way Jesus did, allowing the Holy Spirit to bring change.[212] Everyone is a sinner (Rom 3:23). James adds that missing the mark by a lot or a little is still a sin (James 2:10). The sin of acting on a same-sex attraction is no greater or lesser than any other sin and can be forgiven. Forgiveness and a fresh start are available to all who seek it (1 John 1:9). New life through the Holy Spirit is offered to all who come to Jesus (Gal 5:16-26). Argument and debate will not win this group to the cause of Jesus Christ. Being the hands, feet, heart, and eyes of Jesus is the starting point. Presenting Jesus as the source of hope, help, and healing is a first step and is crucial to impact this diverse group of people.

A Different Response to Same-Sex Attraction

There is an approach that some have taken to this struggle that is worth noting. What can one do who wants to follow Jesus, believes in the Bible, and yet struggles with homosexual feelings? Wesley Hill provides an answer. Hill asserts the Christian's struggle with homosexuality is not unique. Sin, mercy, and forgiveness are the same for all humans, regardless of the temptation.[213] The struggles of those with same-sex attraction are not particularly different than the struggles of heterosexual people. The Christian's responsibility is to be pure and holy. For those who have same-sex attractions, Hill advocates for a life of celibacy.[214] This response is similar to that of the heterosexual single person. What was especially powerful in Hill's book is his stark admission, "What I wish, is that I could feel the church to be a safe place."[215] That desire resonates. For the admittedly small number of people who wrestle with same-sex attractions and battle to not act upon them, this is a real concern. Will the church be a place where they can fight that fight? Choosing celibacy is not likely to receive wide approval in culture, but it is biblical. One of the most important truths that can be shared is that self-worth is not determined by sexuality. Human beings are much more than their sexuality. Today's culture seems to make sexuality the defining issue, but today's culture is wrong.

One of the biggest questions surrounding same-sex attraction is whether it is genetic or a choice. While many Christians believe that same-sex attractions are a choice, Hill makes the case that same-sex attraction may be one of the results of the fall.[216] This is something that those who seek to minister to this group should consider. It may be part of a human's sin nature that some wrestle with same-sex attractions. This understanding connects with the assertion among biologists who suggest same-sex attraction in humans is partly genetic,[217] and provides a common platform from which a discussion can begin.

What About the "T" of LGBT?

This chapter has primarily focused on same-sex attractions and the homosexual lifestyle. While that remains a big issue for Christians today, the "T" of the LGBT movement is prominent as well. How can we minister to the transgender community? Do they even want to be ministered to? The Springtide Research Institute reports that less than one in five Gen Z students who identify as non-binary are connected to a religious group.[218] In 2015, a major poll of transgender people was conducted that revealed some startling statistics. The survey showed that sixty-six percent of the survey respondents (all transgender people) were, at one point in their lives, connected to a faith community.[219] The same survey reveals that nearly one in five transgender people leave their faith community, and that most transgender people that want to be a part of a faith community do so in a church that affirms that lifestyle.[220]

For those who hold to the truth and authority of Scripture, ministering to this group is not an easy task. The principles that apply to those in same-sex relationships, also apply here. To those who don't know Jesus, the message is "Jesus loves you and died for you." Pointing them to Jesus and sharing the truth of God's Word (this lifestyle is not one that honors God) is a tough, but necessary challenge. We also have to realize that those who do want a spiritual component in their lives will likely go to a church that affirms the way they want to live. It is difficult to reach this group as a whole, but those who are engaged in the community may meet individuals with whom a relationship can be built. Reaching the whole group seems daunting but reaching one may be possible.

I once received an unusual phone call. The daughter-in-law of one of our church families wanted to meet with me. When she came in, she told me she and her husband were getting divorced. She was leaving him and her two children because she believed she was not a woman. She believed her true identity was as a man. That was not something I had encountered before. I mostly listened to her. I talked some about what the Bible said and how God created her, and Jesus loved her. After about an hour, I prayed with her. I offered to meet again before she began taking hormones. She was polite but declined to meet. I did not hear from her again for a while. The divorce happened and we tried to minister to the family. I was stunned that about a year later, she contacted me. She identified herself as a "she." She told me that she appreciated our talk, but more than anything, those who prayed for her. She stopped taking the hormones and did not progress with any surgery. Though she thanked me, I am certain nothing I said had much to do with it. She encountered Jesus and the Holy Spirit. That's what brought about the transformation. While she and her husband did not reconcile, they have a good relationship, and she is a good mother to her children. I share this because the task of reaching this group seems so hard and there is so little change. However, one person can change. Prayer and bringing people to Jesus can make all the difference.

Summing Up

The issue of same-sex attraction is real and one that will continue to challenge people in the coming years. Successful ministry across lines of difference must be anchored to the truth of God's Word. The Bible, as the inerrant Word of God and, as such, must be held as the authority. Despite those in the church community who want to make the Bible say something else, those who minister across lines of difference must hold to the truths it plainly states. Acting on same-sex attraction is against what God desires. It is a sin. It is not a greater sin, nor a lesser sin. It is, however, sin. Living a transgender lifestyle is not what God wants for his children. Holding truth, though, does not mean hate. The response to those who wrestle with same-sex attraction issues or transgender issues should be one of compassion. It is the combination of truth bathed in love and caring. It is the same compassion Jesus showed to the woman caught in adultery. It is the response of the father regarding his prodigal son in Jesus' parable. Ministry to those with same-sex attractions or transgender issues is hard. The answer for all who struggle in these areas is the universal one. People need Jesus Christ. Effective ministry will not likely provide impetus or conviction for someone to alter his or her conduct. Only Jesus can do that. The most impactful thing those who minister to these groups of people can do is point them to the Lord. May it be the goal of ministry to this group that all come to a similar place described by Hill: "My shorthand description for this place of tension I was (and am) seeking to occupy is 'washed and waiting'— forgiven and cleansed in the waters of baptism, per Paul's description in 1 Corinthians 6, and eagerly awaiting the redemption of the body, with the final sanctification and transformation of a fallen sexuality."[221]

Chapter 10

Biblical Justice

The evening of May 25, 2020, is a date that is etched into the collective consciousness of the American psyche. On that day, a white Minneapolis police officer in the process of arresting George Floyd, a black man, knelt on his neck for almost ten minutes. Floyd died. His death, recorded by bystanders, ignited what was one the largest protest movements in U.S. history and sparked a nationwide debate on policing and justice.

The discussion of justice was dominant throughout the spring and summer of 2020. The call for justice, though, is not new. In the spring of 2023, eighty-eight-year-old Carolyn Bryant Donham passed away in a small town in Louisiana. What some may not know is that Carolyn Bryant was the woman who, in 1955, falsely accused Emmit Till of acting inappropriately toward her leading to his brutal death. Remarkably, Bryant's husband and his half-brother were found not guilty of the heinous murder. Calls for justice went unheard at that time, even though the pair later confessed the crime to a magazine reporter.[222]

Injustice has reared its ugly head before. Students of history will be aware of what have been called the "Tulsa Race Riots." Following World War I, Tulsa, Oklahoma, was recognized nationally for its wealthy African American community known as the Greenwood District. The Greenwood District was a place where businesses thrived. The whole area became known as the "Black Wall Street." On the morning of May 30, 1921, a young black man named Dick Rowland was riding in the elevator in the Drexel Building with a white woman named Sarah Page. Page accused Rowland of acting inappropriately and threateningly to her. The story was picked up by *The Tulsa Tribune,* who wrote an inflammatory account which fired up both the black and white communities. Many white people were outraged and looking for revenge. Black people feared another lynching. Mobs formed at the courthouse. Rowland was arrested. This led to gunshots being fired. On the next day, June 1, white rioters burned down the Greenwood District. The National Guard was called in and over six thousand blacks were arrested or detained, some for as many as eight days.[223] A 2001 Race Riot Commission determined that Black Tulsans had every reason to believe that Dick Rowland would be lynched after his arrest. His charges were later dismissed. The truth is that they were highly suspect from the start. None of the acts of criminal violence or destruction of property were ever punished.[224] Honest calls for justice were muted in 1921.

Justice matters. Currently, demands for justice are much louder and occasionally much different. Sometimes they do not demand correction for an individual circumstance but instead echo an old cry of the oppressed throwing off the oppressor. At times, cries for justice today come dressed in the clothing of critical theory. Kevin Watson asserts, "Critical theory functions as part of a comprehensive worldview. On the basis of this worldview, people who accept critical theory then interpret the world through this particular lens (oppressed and oppressors), as opposed to others."[225] This construct inflames many protests and protesters today. The cries for justice sometimes arise in an "us vs. them" construct. Sandee LaMotte, a reporter for CNN online, writes about an interview with social justice educator Robin DiAngelo. In that interview, she notes DiAngelo's statement, "If you're a white person in America, you're a racist, pure and simple, and without a lifetime of conscious effort you always will be."[226] Is the only path to justice through the road of the oppressed and oppressor dynamic? Is the only path to justice through this warped view of social justice? Is there another way, a biblical way to examine justice and how to see it prevail?

Ministry across lines of racial, cultural, and socio-economic lines must deal with the issue of biblical justice and what that phrase means. To address this issue, it is vital to see what the Bible says regarding God's view of justice. Isaiah 1:17 describes what the Lord wants from His people: "Learn to do right; seek justice. Defend the oppressed. Take up the cause of the fatherless and plead the case for the widow." Proverbs 31:8-9 indicates that God's people are to be concerned about injustice around them: "Speak up for those who cannot speak for themselves, for the rights of all who are destitute. Speak up and judge fairly; defend the rights of the poor and needy." It is clear from these passages and others (Lev 19:5, Deut 10:17-18, Psalm 10:17-18, Psalm 33:5, Amos 5:21-24, and Luke 11:42) that God desires that His people actively seek justice in the world in which they live.

What is Biblical Justice?

God wants his people to champion justice, so that leads to the question, what is justice according to the Bible? There are three aspects of biblical justice that manifest themselves in two distinct ways. Biblical justice has three distinct components: distributive, retributive, and restorative. These three attributes are to be practiced both individually and collectively. The importance of understanding and exhibiting biblical justice cannot be overstated. It is the lens by which Christians view God's actions and commands and the framework by which we evaluate human behavior.

The Three Components of Biblical Justice

The first attribute of biblical justice is distributive justice. This aspect of justice highlights the fair allocation of resources within the community and ensures that all people have access to what they need to live. The Bible is clear about how God's people were to practice distributive justice. God told his people, "When you reap the harvest of your land, do not reap to the very edges of your field, or gather the gleanings of your harvest. Do not go over your vineyard a second time or pick up the grapes that have fallen. Leave them for the poor and the foreigner. I am the Lord your God" (Lev 19:9-10). The "Year of Jubilee," mentioned in Leviticus 25 is another way God wanted his people to be committed to distributive justice. The New Testament also speaks of distributive justice. In Acts 6, one of the first challenges of the early church was the problem of caring for widows. The Hellenistic Jews were unhappy that their widows were being neglected. The disciples resolved that issue by appointing seven men to make sure that resources were properly distributed to all the widows. James also indicates the importance of making sure the neglected have what they need: "Religion that God our Father accepts as pure and faultless is this: to look after orphans and widows in their distress and to keep oneself from being polluted by the world" (James 1:27).

The second attribute of biblical justice is retributive justice. Retributive justice is about punishment proportionate to the offense committed. The aim of retributive justice is to correct wrongdoing. It seeks to ensure that the punishment fits the crime. The most commonly used passage describing retributive justice is Exodus 21:23-25: "If people are fighting and hit a pregnant woman and she gives birth prematurely but there is no serious injury, the offender must be fined whatever the woman's husband demands, and the court allows. But if there is serious injury, you are to take life for life, eye for eye, tooth for tooth, hand for hand, foot for foot, burn for burn, wound for wound, bruise for bruise." Sometimes, in today's culture, these verses are misapplied to define vengeance or revenge. That is not how they should be understood. These verses are there to make sure that punishment is just and appropriate for the situation. Another passage that demonstrates retributive justice is Genesis 9:6: "Whoever sheds human blood, by humans shall their blood be shed, for in the image of God has God made mankind." These verses indicate the seriousness with which God views sin and how it impacts his people.

The final attribute of biblical justice is restorative justice. This is an aspect of justice that is often overlooked by today's cultural warriors. It emphasizes the restoration of relationships beyond just retribution. Its aim is to restore right standing with God and with those who have been wronged. Restorative justice is the core message of the gospel and emphasizes healing and transformation. One of the best examples of restorative justice in the New Testament is Jesus' parable of the prodigal son found in Luke 15. The youngest son foolishly leaves his father, taking his inheritance with him. He squanders it and comes to realize he is not worthy of being a son anymore. He decides that going home as a servant is better than the lifestyle he's living, so he makes his way home. The father, who's been watching for him to return the whole time, sees him coming and runs to meet him. He not only forgives him but restores him to his position and celebrates. The heart of restorative justice is the mending of broken relationships, hearts, and lives.

Individually and in Community

Biblical justice is to be seen in both the individual and the community. Justice is the responsibility of the individual Christian. This particular aspect is not discussed as much in culture today. For the individual, justice is "living in right relationship with others—with God, and with human beings made in His image. It defines how a person ought to treat others—what kind of behavior is good and right and what is not."[227] One of the key passages in describing biblical justice at a personal level is Micah 6:8: "He has shown you, O mortal, what is good. And what does the Lord require of you? To act justly and to love mercy and to walk humbly with your God." Timothy Keller writes of this verse, "The term for 'mercy' is the Hebrew word *chesedh*, God's unconditional grace and compassion. The word for "justice" is the Hebrew word *misphat*. In Micah 6:8 *misphat* puts the emphasis on action. *Chesedh* puts it on the attitude or motive of the action." Simply put; to walk with God, we must do justice out of merciful love.[228] Walter J. Houston equates justice with fairness.[229]

Distributive justice demands that each Christian do his/her part in making sure that those in need have the opportunity to have their needs met. Retributive justice calls each Christian to stand for truth and oppose actions that harm other people. Christians of all ethnicities must speak out for those whom culture has muted their voices. Whether the group be homeless, poverty-stricken, disadvantaged, or unborn, Christians across lines of difference must stand to defend and protect the innocent. Restorative justice also has a place in the life of the individual Christian. Christians of all different backgrounds must seek healing, forgiveness, and love with those with whom it has not been easy to connect. Treating others equally and recognizing that all people are made in the image of God are critical components of biblical justice.

Biblical justice is also a community responsibility. It begins with the recognition that all people are created "Imago Dei" (God's image). This is a vital truth on which an individual Christian's life is built and the foundation upon which the community's values stand. There is not a person on the planet that does not merit the love and respect that is due someone for whom Jesus died. That respect leads to a need to treat all people fairly. Jesus' words resonate as he said, "So in everything, do to others what you would have them do to you, for this sums up the Law and the Prophets" (Matt 7:12). Collectively, when Christians hold themselves to this level of individual accountability, personal encounters and interactions get closer to God's desire for justice.

The community has a responsibility to ensure distributive justice. Historically, churches have done this through the building of hospitals, children's homes, and food kitchens. These kinds of endeavors must continue. As people continue to struggle, the church's opportunity to love and serve continues to grow. Of the early church, it was said, "there was not a needy person among them" (Acts 4:34). How much impact would that have if that was said of churches today?

In addition to distributive justice, the church, as a body, has a responsibility to stand for retributive justice. This begins with the understanding that one of the responsibilities of leaders is to reward good conduct and punish inappropriate conduct. Allen argues that this kind of justice "is reserved for God-ordained authorities—including parents in the home, pastors in the church, and civil authorities in the state." He asserts that this kind of justice demands that authorities judge fairly and treat everyone equally before the law because that is how God treats people. He impartially rewards the good and punishes the wrong.[230] Retributive justice does not allow mistreatment of a particular individual or group. Retributive justice demands corrective action when those in authority have ignored their responsibilities and abused their powers. Retributive justice is what is often meant when people demand "justice" in today's culture. It is important that the church has a voice at the table with respect to retributive justice. Historically, the church has played a big role in the major ethical and moral decisions of our country. For example, consider the abolitionist movement. It is sometimes overlooked that the roots of the abolitionist movement are found deep in the Christian faith. "One reason abolitionists are forgotten is that they were inescapably Christian in their motives, means, and vocabulary. Not that all abolitionists were orthodox Christians, though a large proportion were."[231]

Consider the rights of children with respect to work and education. In the 1830's in England, thousands of children were compelled daily to work in the Yorkshire worsted mills for eleven hours a day with only one thirty-minute break. This outraged many. As this situation became known, Christians, especially a group of Yorkshire evangelicals, began working diligently for reform.[232] In this country and around the world, Christians have been willing to speak up for those treated unjustly.

The last way the community can demonstrate biblical justice is to have a commitment to restorative justice. This is the desire and commitment to walk together with brothers and sisters in Christ recognizing that the things which unite are far greater than the things that might be used to divide. Restorative justice is what can bring healing, health, and hope to our fractured culture. Restorative justice is connected with reconciliation, both with God and with other people. Forgiveness is at the heart of restorative justice. A powerfully poignant example of that occurred in Charleston, South Carolina in 2015. Many of the family members of the victims of Dylan Roof's shooting spoke words of forgiveness at his sentencing hearing. It was an act that sought to bring hope and healing to fractured racial relations in that community and beyond. Restorative justice is the third facet of biblical justice that seeks to connect people with each other and to connect them with the Lord.

Different Worldviews

The call for justice has grown louder over the last decade. The idea of biblical justice has emerged in the discussion. However, the phrase used most often in cultural discussions is "social justice." The phrase "social justice" is one that evokes different reactions from a wide range of people. Many churches historically have used the term to mean biblical justice. There are many Christians who are committed to seeing the Lord's will be done "on earth as it is in heaven." The desire to seek justice is commendable and honors the Lord. However, there is a segment of people (the progressive church and many in the community) that sees a different view of "social justice" than that of the Bible.

Worldview of the Oppressed and the Oppressors

There are two different worldviews that demand justice in today's culture. The first is a worldview that does not recognize a sovereign God. It views the world through the lens of the oppressed and the oppressor. It is a philosophy that goes by many names, but it is the philosophy that has inspired many protest movements and is rooted in Marxism. For many, the term "Social Justice" means supporting and recognizing the oppressed and opposing oppressors. Good, in this worldview, are the oppressed people. Evil, in this worldview, is the oppressive systems and those that are oppressors. In this view, people are often not seen as individuals but as part of a people group. Individual identity is inseparable from the group identity. People are either "oppressed" or "the oppressor." Allen contends that this view of social justice, as it is often defined politically, is a worldview that is opposed to a biblical worldview.[233] He notes that this kind of justice "seeks the overthrow of systemic white supremacy, the patriarchy, and Judeo-Christian morality."[234] While eliminating white supremacy and racism is good and a right ambition, Allen argues that this viewpoint is not biblical: "There is only grievance, condemnation, and retribution. Bigots, haters, and oppressors must be destroyed."[235] This is a justice that does not see all people created in the image of God. Instead, it sees those in power oppressing those who are not. This is a justice that does not seek repentance, forgiveness, and reconciliation. It seeks the destruction of the group in power to empower the powerless. It demands people be canceled for wrong thinking or conduct. It is a version of justice that does not have room for transformation. It is a justice that demands virtue-signaling over substance. This kind of justice requires people to be divided into groups and not viewed as an individual made in the image of God. Allen quotes Scott Aniol of Southwestern Baptist Theological Seminary as he writes, "No thoughtful Christian approves of true racism, injustice, or oppression when it exists. But, by adopting these secular, leftist categories, which are rooted in ideologies explicitly intended to divide people, well-meaning Christians are making divides within Christianity and even broader society worse rather than better."[236]

God-Centered Worldview

A second form of justice comes from a different worldview. This worldview is God-centered and sees the events and actions of humanity under his authority. For those who see the reality of a sovereign God and absolute truth, biblical justice involves recognizing all people as image-bearers of God. It demands unfairness and mistreatment be addressed because they are sinful and violate the way that a holy God wants human beings to live and interact with each other. This view of justice recognizes "everyone has God-given endowments—a creative mind, a heart, hands, a unique personality, and gifts."[237] This worldview seeks ways to equip victims to be victorious. This view of justice recognizes and celebrates the different aspects of each person's story and identity without making differences the defining factor. It seeks to unify based on shared common truth, genuine repentance, and the possibility of reconciliation. This view of justice demands more than just external, societal change. Its purpose is to change hearts. Allen writes, "The problems with the world are not out there in society; rather, they are in here in our fallen hearts and minds."[238]

To address injustice in a biblical way, Christians must choose to act. Practically, it means that churches must address cultural issues as they arise but do so in the context of sin and repentance. This view of justice demands standing up for those wrongly treated because God stands for the powerless (Ps 146:7-9). This view of justice calls the church to be a voice for holiness and righteousness when the voices of hate and division are often the loudest. This view of justice calls for the church to be the change agent when institutions have trampled upon those who are easily ignored. The goal of this kind of justice is reconciliation (man to God and man to man), righteousness (seeing what is right and justice done), and truth (not acquiescing to strong political winds one way or the other). This understanding of biblical justice is important and must be a part of ministering across lines of difference.

Overview of the Justice Question

Handling the issue of biblical justice is critical if the church is going to continue to be relevant in the lives of people. Justice cannot be separated from a person's relationship with God. Sin separated humanity from the Father (Isa 59:2). It is only through the atoning sacrifice of Jesus that justification can be found (Acts 13:39). A right relationship with God enables the believer to live in right relationship with others. Biblical justice should be a part of the DNA of the Christian in the twenty-first century. Social justice and Biblical justice will continue to compete in the public arena. While there are many progressive churches that have adopted the cultural view of social justice rooted in Marxism, churches who respect the authority of Scripture cannot do that. Biblical justice is rooted in the truth of Scripture. Allen describes it this way, "We, the Bible-believing church, must quickly relearn from our forebears what genuine Christian mission should be. We need to recover that older theology that seamlessly links the gospel, evangelism, and discipleship with faithfully living out the implications of a biblical worldview in every area of life." [239]

Summing Up

Biblical justice is the responsibility of all who wear the name of Jesus Christ. We have to be committed to distributive, retributive, and restorative justice as it is explained in the Bible. God's character is just. "He rules the world in righteousness and judges the peoples with equity" (Ps.9:8). The challenge to determine what situations call Christians to speak out and which are matters of cultural opinion or discussion is real, and requires grace, love, and patience for all who wrestle with it. While it is a tough challenge, it is one that cannot be ignored. We cannot ignore the possibility of being asked what we did while terrible acts were being committed. The justice issue was brought home to me in a personal way in 2013. At the time, I served in a local church and volunteered at a juvenile correctional facility. I was asked by the chaplain at that facility to do Bible Bowl with the young men incarcerated there, and I agreed to do it. We met for almost a year before the state of Ohio changed chaplains and removed religious programming. In late December of 2013, my program was discontinued. Until that time, I enjoyed working with those young men. We did Bible Bowl on Sunday afternoons. Then, I was asked to do a study session with some of them once a week. I did a few church services with them, too. The ages of the inmates ranged from eleven to twenty-one.

I noticed that over eighty percent of the young men there were African American. When I asked the chaplain about the disproportionate number of African Americans, he told me that the guys in the facility, black, white, and Hispanic, came from lower income families. He also told me that very few of the young men there were wrongly imprisoned. They were there because they broke the law. What he said next stuck with me. He said that many other kids, a majority of them white kids, who had committed the same crimes were not there. Their families had the means to keep them out of doing time. The young men in that facility, mostly African Americans, were not wrongly imprisoned. They did what they were accused of doing. They did time because, in many cases, their families did not have the tools available to them to manage the system. This observation highlighted what I think I already knew. The legal system in the United States, though the greatest in the world, is not perfect. May those who wear the name of Jesus never back down from speaking truth and justice. We must have an increased willingness to act. "If anyone, then, knows the good they ought to do and doesn't do it, it is sin for them" (James 4:17).

Chapter 11

Nobody's Home

There is a growing segment of the population of the United States that needs to be addressed by those who minister across lines of racial, cultural, and socio-economic differences. In 2022, it was reported that there were 7.7 million latchkey kids in the United States. That doubles the amount from 2000.[240] Additionally, in 2022, there were more than 23 million kids living in single parent homes, which was about one in every three children in the country.[241] This area of need impacts all three areas of ministry discussed here. It can cut across racial, cultural, and socio-economic lines of differences. For many young people today, especially though not exclusively in urban areas, when school is over, there is simply nobody home. This is a facet of ministry that demands attention. Jesus said, "Whoever welcomes one such child in my name welcomes me" (Matt. 18:5).

For many of these families, the struggle is not only that of a single parent, but it is also a struggle for resources. Single moms are one of the most disadvantaged groups in the United States. In 2021, thirty-one percent of single-parent families were living below the poverty level.[242] This makes the challenge even greater for almost a third of single-parent families. They are trying to handle the activities of life with only one adult in the home while also dealing with not having enough money to cover expenses. The dual nature of this problem is one that those who seek to minister across lines of difference will inevitably face.

Commitment to the Family

The church is often referred to as the "family of God." Lawrence Richards writes that love, within the body of Christ, is a special mark of family relationship.[243] Paul writes to the church at Rome about how love within the family is demonstrated: "Love must be sincere. Hate what is evil; cling to what is good. Be devoted to one another in love. Honor one another above yourselves. Never be lacking in zeal, but keep your spiritual fervor, serving the Lord. Be joyful in hope, patient in affliction, faithful in prayer. Share with the Lord's people who are in need. Practice hospitality" (Rom. 12:9-13). Paul's appeal here is for followers of Jesus to live out love in a real, personal way. According to Richards, "Paul's careful attention to interpersonal relationships here is not nagging. It is a concerned affirmation of the fact that for transformation to take place, and for conformity to be rejected, the quality of relationships which exist within the church is of vital importance."[244] Simply put, the church has an opportunity to reach out and minister to a growing group of people whose lives are different than what is often viewed as the "normative" Christian family.

The opportunity to minister comes with a responsibility. Churches and ministries can help with basic needs and many already do, which is not a bad thing. However, churches and ministries have the opportunity to do even more. They have the opportunity to give respect. Demonstrating respect to those who need help begins by properly ascertaining the problem. Some may not need money as much as they need a relationship that helps them stay in a job. This is much more difficult, but more rewarding in the long term. It also allows the recipient to gain respect. Ministries and churches that want to help beyond just the tangible, need to move beyond just a "helping in the moment" mindset. It means helping them find ways to provide for themselves and their families. It allows them to do something for what they are being given. People don't really want to be "cases" or "causes." Ministry that can help them be a "contributor" can accomplish more.

Be Aware of the Challenges of Single Parents

In the church culture, because family is stressed (and rightly so), it is easy to forget that not everyone has the same family experience. There are people who have never married and don't have children. There are also single parent families, most often parents and children who have been through a divorce. They do not experience church and family events the same way that others do. Single parents have to deal with sharing parental responsibilities and time. They have to manage having their kids some of the time and sharing holidays. These struggles are real when both parents want a role in their children's lives. Sometimes single parents have to handle it all alone. Linda Ransom Jacobs knows this. She is a Christian woman whose husband left her and their children. In her book, *The Single Parent: Confident and Successful*, she addresses some of the challenges that single parents must confront.

The first of these is loneliness. About attending her children's events at school or church, Jacobs wrote, "I felt like I no longer had a family. It was just the kids and me. There was no one to share the day's events with and no one to talk with about the funny things the kids did or their accomplishments. I felt I was totally alone."[245] That feeling can be difficult for single parents to address. Like other parents, they have work schedules to maintain, children's homework and events to monitor, and bedtimes and bath times to manage. It can be difficult to find the time to find others with whom they can talk or simply relax and enjoy.

A second challenge that single parents wrestle with is raising their children by themselves or with a partner who is not there and does not necessarily do things the same way. This includes discipline, instilling values, and what is and isn't acceptable conduct. Children of single parents may have difficulty exhibiting consistent behaviors. What is acceptable in one home is not acceptable in the other. Single parents can find themselves weary and exasperated by the constant, daunting task of raising children. While all parents know the struggle and challenges of raising children, it is multiplied for those doing it alone or those who have to work together with a distant parent.

A third issue that single parents have to manage is that of needing help and not being willing to ask or not knowing where to ask for it. Jacobs addresses the situation plainly. She writes, "Single parents, for the most part, are an independent group. We have to be in order to survive and parent our children alone. Sometimes it is okay to ask for help. Sometimes it is necessary to ask for help."[246] While asking for help seems like an obvious thing, many times single parents and their children plow through without seeking assistance. As most families know, there are times when a child needs the influence of a dad or the love and nurture of a mom. Children often do better when they have the support of both a dad and a mom. In single parent homes, many times that is not as easy and sometimes just not possible at all. Jacobs observes, "Perhaps you are a dad who needs help finding your daughter a certain dress or costume for a play. Or you are a dad, and your daughter has her first menstrual period. What do you know about shopping for this stuff? Do dads even do this?"[247] They do, but maybe they don't have to do it alone.

These are but three of a myriad of challenges faced by single parents. All parents deal with similar issues, but they don't necessarily have the condition of doing it on their own or balancing it on an every-other-weekend basis. Being aware of what those who are trying to raise children in a different environment face will point out areas in which the church can help.

What Does Ministry to this Group Look Like?

The writer of Hebrews identifies the importance of ministering to those who are struggling: "God is not unjust; he will not forget your work and the love you have shown him as you have helped his people and continue to help them" (Heb. 6:10). God knows and sees ministry that is not often splashed on social media. It is the kind of ministry that gets very little notice at all except for those it involves. It's the kind of ministry that can make a huge difference. What can the church do? How can ministry across lines of difference make an impact in this community?

Ministry to Parents

Serving single parents in any community is a worthwhile ministry that will bear fruit. One of the best ways a ministry can do that is to address the "alone" factor. Many single parents are facing the daunting challenges of family life alone. Additionally, they may be experiencing loneliness and hoping for another adult to talk to and simply share the day. If the people engaged in ministry can develop friendships with single parents, it will help create bonds or ties which can bring people together.

Another way that churches and ministries can reach out to single parents is to schedule events with the single parent family in mind. Carnivals and game nights can be planned to have multiple adults working with kids and making sure they are doing the activities that are set up for them. There are times when ministry event planners assume that parents will manage their children through different aspects of an event. A single parent with more than one child will have a difficult time doing that. Childcare is expensive and difficult to find. Careful planning by ministry leaders can make some ministry events accessible to the single parent family.

Holiday parties and gatherings are another occasion that can be harder for single parents. Ministry event planners can try to coordinate different age groups to do things at a similar time so that the parent doesn't have to find childcare. Sometimes, buying gifts for kids can be tough for parents, especially those in economically challenged areas and those who may be single parents. Ministries can help with this, too. There are many church groups who have adopted families for Christmas and made sure that the children had gifts, and the family had a meal. This is good and well-intentioned. However, there is another way it could be done that could provide more than one gift. It could help ensure a child's Christmas and maintain the dignity of a struggling adult.

Dr. Robert Lupton discovered a way to do just that. In an article written by JoAnne Viviano, Lupton suggested that instead of donating gifts that would be taken to "needy" families, the people in his ministry donate a gift, which they put into a store. Because the items were donated, prices could be cut to an affordable range. Parents in the neighborhood, some though not all single parents, could then come to the store and purchase their own presents for their children at discounted prices. Those who could not afford the discount prices could work at the store to earn money to buy gifts. Lupton's emphasis was on giving the gift of dignity to parents, especially those who were trying to do it all alone. They were able to know the joy that comes from giving to their children at Christmas.[248]

Ministry to Children

Ministry to the children and young people in single parent homes or those kids for whom one or both parents are not around is crucial if this group of people is to be reached. It has the potential to change not only the lives of the children, but the heart of the church, as well. Michael Goheen writes, "When a church becomes deeply involved in the needs of its neighborhood, it changes both the church and the attitude of the local community."[249] There are numerous ways that ministry to this group can occur.

After School Programs

Dick Gruber explains, "Kids who learn to hear God's voice early are more likely to receive His instructions, choose to obey Him, and become His followers for life."[250] Ministry to children and young people makes a difference. One of the best ways to minister to kids in the community is through after school programs. There are many different kinds of after school programs and they are continuing to change and adapt to the current culture. The concept of having public school children get specialized church training began with the concept of "Release Time." As early as 1905, the idea of released-time education in the United States was conceived. A school conference in New York City first discussed the idea. It was proposed at that time for public elementary schools to be closed one day a week, in addition to Sunday, for religious education. This gave parents the option for their children to receive religious instruction outside school grounds with the public school accommodating their schedules for the program. The public school system was not involved in the religious teaching, which was done off campus. The program evolved from being a full day, to the public school allowing an hour in the day, one day a week, for religious teaching. In 1947, there were almost two million public school students participating in a Release Time program. Release Time met some legal challenges in the middle of the twentieth century. Today, Release Time still exists but is not nearly as prevalent.

After school programs are now more common than students being released during the day. After school programs are not all the same. Some are in the tradition of the Release Time concept and teach Bible and Christian values to children who come after school one day a week. Other after school programs incorporate tutoring and working with students in academic areas. There may be some spiritual component, but the program is geared to help the student finish what many students finish with parents at home. Some after school programs include a snack for the children, and a few of them even provide the evening meal.

Though there are different approaches to how a ministry might want to approach doing an after-school program, there is no denying the success of such a program. In the mid-1990's, the church where I was serving in Kansas City, Kansas, decided to create an after-school program with the elementary school across the street from us. There was a process we had to follow to make this happen. We received permission from the Kansas City, Kansas, school superintendent and the principal of our neighborhood school. This was not hard to get, and both were excited for our church to partner with kids in the neighborhood. It was agreed that we would have parent permission forms distributed to the kids at school. Parents would have to give permission for their students to attend each Wednesday afternoon. They would also need to agree to pick up their children at 5:15 in the evening. Once these preliminaries were covered, we began the program. We got volunteers from the church to lead classes. We followed a "Release Time" format in that our primary focus was on Christian teaching and values. We had a worship time, a class time, a game time, snack time, and a craft time. It was, in many ways, a weekly Vacation Bible School. We called it "Weekday Church School" and it was a regular part of our church for many years. Over the nearly ten years we had the program, we interacted with nearly one hundred children in our neighborhood and their parents. There were many positive things that occurred through the Weekday Church School program. We had the opportunity to get to know many kids in our neighborhood and their families. We saw them each week, had conversations with them, and developed friendships. We knew when they had problems and could reach out to help. We did that with a few bills that a single parent could not pay. We were able to visit one of our kid's grandmothers in the hospital. We became a part of their lives, and they became a part of ours. Some of the people in the neighborhood came to our church and some did not. However, our outreach and our family grew.

Special Interests Camps

Another potential way for churches and church groups to reach young people who may not have parents at home is to have special interest camps after school or on a weekend. These kinds of camps can include sports, drama, art, or music. While there are groups that can help a church or ministry put on one of these camps, these can often be managed and staffed by those in the church or ministry.

Sports camps can include basketball, baseball, volleyball, soccer, flag football, taekwondo, and cheerleading/dance. The emphasis of these sports camps is to familiarize young people with a sport of their choosing and provide them quality instruction on how to play the sport with integrity and character. These kinds of camps also provide a wonderful opportunity for mentorship. The camps can be structured, depending on the location and the time, to include a time of worship and a healthy snack. Because of the athletic nature of these camps, nutrition and good eating habits can also be taught.

Music, art, and drama camps operate the same way as the sports camp. Young people sign up for a particular facet of the camp and the church leaders and volunteers can lead different sessions. For an art camp, the goal at the end of the camp can be to have an art exhibition for those in the neighborhood, the church, and the parents. The music camp can work together to prepare a presentation for the neighborhood, church, and parents. The drama camp can put on a play or musical that can be done during the Sunday worship time. These kinds of camps serve young people in areas that they find interesting. They allow students to do things that they might not normally get to do and to learn it at a higher level than was previously possible. The key benefit is that a ministry or church provides opportunities that some children may never receive, while demonstrating the love of Jesus.

Vacation Bible School

The Vacation Bible School has a wonderful opportunity to introduce children to Jesus Christ, provide them a nurturing, caring environment, and allow them to have fun. I found it interesting that Vacation Bible Schools were begun in New York City in 1901 by the Rev. Robert G. Boville in the slums of the city.[251] The purpose was to reach children that were overlooked, and many times, unreached. The goal in 1901 remains the same today. One of the basic ways a ministry can impact single-parent families and impoverished areas is to offer a Vacation Bible School, free of charge for the neighborhood kids.

Having a Vacation Bible School can bring many blessings to a community. VBS is one of the most reliable ways to bring together a church or ministry and engage a variety of ages in the same task. It allows the church to work together to accomplish a meaningful goal. VBS provides children with an opportunity to experience an engaging and fun environment with caring adults. Those who volunteer in VBS have the chance to interact with kids and demonstrate kindness, patience, and care. Vacation Bible School also gives the ministry an opportunity to build a foundation of faith and biblical truth for the young people who attend. Children are exposed to all kinds of things and many of them are not Godly or positive. VBS gives a church or ministry the opportunity to counter those messages. One of the most important benefits for the kids, especially in difficult areas or situations, is that VBS can foster a sense of belonging.

Choosing to offer a VBS to minister across lines of difference is a powerful way to make a difference in the lives of children and benefit families, especially single parents, in the neighborhood. "The purpose of Christian education, broadly defined, is disciple-making through a wide-ranging spectrum of teaching."[252] For many kids in challenging situations, the Vacation Bible School remains one of the most impactful ways to disciple.

Summing Up

Ministry to those who sometimes fall through the cracks is vital. For ministry across lines of racial, cultural, and socio-economic differences, to be successful, noticing the neglected matters. God's desire is for all people to come to him. "Abraham will surely become a great and powerful nation, and all nations on earth will be blessed through him" (Genesis 18:18). This reveals God's intent from the beginning, that all people have worth and value. He wants all people to live with him forever. Psalm 98:3 notes, "He has remembered his love and his faithfulness to Israel; all the ends of the earth have seen the salvation of our God." If that is God's desire, expressed from the beginning, how can we not promote reaching out to all the people around us? As noted earlier, Jesus challenged the disciples in Matthew 28:19-20. Michael E. Green writes of this passage, "That is a very comprehensive commission. It represents Christ's standing orders for his church. Unfortunately, many churches in the West have to a large extent neglected it. Congregations and clergy seem committed to maintenance, not to mission."[253]

With respect to children and parents in difficult situations, maintenance is not the answer. The church has a unique and wonderful opportunity to demonstrate the love, grace, compassion, and understanding that Jesus offers. If the church is willing to do so, she can be the hands and feet of Jesus to those in need. The imperative is clear. Jesus said, 'Truly I tell you, whatever you did for one of the least of these brothers and sisters of mine, you did for me" (Matthew 25:40). Roger Gench describes Christians with this passion: "They also wanted to take ethics by the horns and do something about the plights of urban areas to contribute in some way to the mending of creation."[254] Ministry that reaches across lines of difference is driven to make a difference, to see change in the lives of people.

The Bible supports the idea of lasting change starting with a relationship with Jesus. He desires that with all people. It comes down to the initial choice about Jesus. "Here I am! I stand at the door and knock. If anyone hears my voice and opens the door, I will come in and eat with that person, and they with me" (Rev 3:20). Ministries that challenge people with that initial, major decision do more for people than they realize. While there are other important issues and decisions, none are more important than that.

Chapter 12

Why It Matters

Being a part of God's kingdom is the most important citizenship anyone will ever have. Through the atoning work of Jesus Christ, God has invited all people of every ethnicity to be with him forever. Receiving an invitation is exciting. Being a part of something that is bigger than you can be thrilling.

I learned what it meant to be wanted and not wanted through high school athletics. My brothers were good athletes, but I, the oldest, was just not as good. I tried hard and I wanted desperately to be a part of the team. It reached a crescendo when I was a freshman in high school. Tryouts for the freshman basketball team were held for a week. I was eager and excited to earn a spot on the team. As I remember, there were sixteen or seventeen guys trying out, so only a handful would be cut. That was a tough week. I went to class during the day, and for a little more than two hours after school, I gave all I had in the drills and scrimmages. I did not make the basketball team in seventh grade but played on a recreational league team. I was certain I had improved. We finished the tryout on Thursday afternoon and were told the list of players would be posted in the locker room the next morning. I was bused to my high school, so the long ride was even longer. We finally got there, and I made my way to the locker room. There were already four or five guys standing around near the list. I slowly approached the list and looked. I scanned all the names. It wasn't there. My name was not on the list. I remember the disappointment and the hurt. My name wasn't there. I didn't make the cut.

The next year our school started a baseball program. Again, I was excited. It was clear that I would not be a basketball player, but I'd played baseball for a long time. I wanted to be part of the team, so I attended the tryouts. The baseball tryouts, like basketball, lasted about a week. There were almost twenty-five guys trying out, but they were keeping about eighteen, so I had a chance. I went through that week of workouts. We caught fly balls, took batting practice, and did infield and throwing practice. I thought I'd done okay as the last day of the tryouts ended. Lots of guys were better than me. I thought I might be better than a couple. A few of the guys missed a day or two. I thought that might help. The list would be posted the next day in the biology teacher's room. He was the assistant coach. Again, it was a long bus ride that morning. When we finally got to school, I went immediately to the classroom. Guys were standing by the list again. I strained to see the names there. They were listed alphabetically. There toward the bottom was the name "Bill Thomas." I made the team. I was chosen to be a part of the group. I'd like to say that led to a brilliant high school, college, and professional career. It didn't. I saw very little action and ended up with a high school batting average of .250. It was fun though. Being chosen to be a part of the team felt really good.

"There's nothing like feeling included." That's the desire of all human beings. Regardless of our differences, we are not like Charlie Brown. In the 1965 *Peanuts: A Charlie Brown Christmas*, Charlie Brown is sad that his mailbox contained no Christmas cards. All of us have received a card, an invitation if you will. All are wanted. All are called to be a part of the kingdom of God. "God is faithful; by him you were called into the fellowship of his Son, Jesus Christ our Lord" (1 Cor 1:9). The word translated "called" can also be understood as "invited." All of humanity is invited to be a part of the kingdom of God. It is our task to let them know.

What Does It Impact?

It's an old preacher story but I think it makes a good point. Some seminary students loved to play basketball. Since the school they attended had no gym, the guys played basketball in a nearby public school. Whenever they played an elderly janitor waited patiently until they were finished. Often, he read his Bible while waiting. One day one of the young men asked him what he was reading. The man answered, 'The book of Revelation.' Surprised that he was reading something so difficult, the seminary student asked if he understood it. 'Oh, yes,' the man assured him. 'I understand it.' 'What does it mean?' Quietly the janitor answered, "It means that Jesus is going to win." Is there any better summary than that? That's the message the church must give to all ethnic groups.

Ministry across lines of racial, cultural, and socio-economic lines of difference is important for the church of the twenty-first century if she is to fulfill her mission. Jesus prayed for those who believed through the message of the apostles: That all of them may be one, Father, just as you are in me, and I am in you. May they also be in us so that the world may believe that you have sent me. I have given them the glory that you gave me, that they may be one as we are one. I in them and you in me—so that they may be brought to complete unity. Then the world will know that you sent me and have loved them even as you have loved me. Father, I want those you have given me to be with me where I am, and to see my glory, the glory you have given me because you loved me before the creation of the world (John 17:20-24).

The events described in John 17, happen just a short time before Jesus' crucifixion. The things he prayed revealed something about what he cared for and what he thought was important. One of those things was a prayer for unity. He asked his Father to empower the disciples and those who would come after them to be united. A glance at this passage reveals three important reasons why it matters that we reach across lines of difference.

Our Walk

The first of these is ministry across lines of difference strengthens our walk with Jesus. The word "walk" refers to living out the Christian faith on a daily basis. The world today struggles with the idea of unity. Jesus prayed for his followers that he would be in them so that they would have "complete unity" (v. 23). Literally, this phrase is "perfected in unity." Jesus indicates that maturity for his followers includes a sense of unity and oneness with brothers and sisters in Christ. Looking at how things are today, there is work to be done.

Who is My Neighbor?

In 2020, Gallup did a poll that indicated that only 44% of Americans believed that race relations between "White and Black Americans" were "good."[255] In 2024, the United States is still wrestling with the issues of affirmative action, reparations, and voting rights. Protests about the wars in Gaza and Ukraine still arise. These issues continue to be discussed in barber shops, on sidewalks, at kitchen tables, on college campuses, and in the halls of Congress. The need for Christians to engage the divided culture has never been greater. Christians in the twenty-first century must reflect the heart of Jesus. Ministry across lines of racial, cultural, and socio-economic difference indicates a longing to take Jesus to places where the world is broken. Jesus specializes in taking that which is broken and healing it, making it right. Our walk is impacted by how we view this ministry. If we are to mature and be what Jesus prayed, we will need a renewed commitment to the Lord to minister to those around us.

Our Worship

The second aspect Jesus notes in his prayer is our worship. In verse 22, John records Jesus praying, "I have given them the glory that you gave me." He continues in verse 24, "I want those you have given me to be with me where I am, and to see my glory, the glory you have given me." Merrill Tenney writes with respect to seeing his glory: "*See* in this context means more than just recognize by form. Observe would be a better translation."[256] Jesus' desire, in this prayer, is for his followers to see him as he really is. Observing or recognizing the glory of Jesus; not a bad description of what it means to worship. Jesus gave his disciples his glory (the opportunity to share in the message of eternal life), so that they may be united. For us today, we have the opportunity to share in his glory (proclaiming the message) and observe his glory (worship) in a way that brings people together.

Worship should be a time for all kinds of different people to unite on the one thing that matters more than anything else. What does it look like in today's church? The answer is a mixed result. In 2020 it was reported that twenty percent of Christian churches (in the broadest sense of the word) were categorized as "multi-ethnic."[257] Remember, a multi-ethnic church is one in which no ethnic group is more than eighty percent of the congregation and a church that seeks to engage in more than one culture. There are more multi-ethnic churches now than previously. That's good news. More American Christians than before are worshipping with brothers and sisters of different backgrounds.

There is a challenge, too. Most Americans who attend church still do so at a church that is predominantly one ethnic group. More than half of the country's Hispanic Protestants attend a multi-ethnic church, but about three in four white and black protestants attend a church consisting of predominantly of one ethnicity.[258] Most American Christians still worship regularly with people that are similar to them. While there has been great progress and there are several amazing, multi-ethnic churches, there is still room for growth.

Our Witness

The third area that reaching across lines of racial, cultural, and socio-economic differences affects, is our witness for the Lord Jesus Christ. If the body of Christ can come together, being "perfected in unity," then, according to Jesus, "the world will know that you sent me and have loved them even as you have loved me" (John 17:21). Unity of the body of Christ authenticates Jesus' nature, person, and work. It also demonstrates to the world that God loves them. It was on Jesus' heart and mind that his followers be one. He wanted the world to see that the church was one even as the Father and Son were one. Unity in the Body of Christ can be a powerful statement to the divided and fragmented world we live in. Jesus is praying for his followers, that as he lives in them and those who come after them, unity will not be the product of hard labor but the outcome of walking closely with him. Simply put, those who walk closely with Jesus can't help but want to walk closely with all brothers and sisters in Christ, regardless of racial, cultural, or socio-economic backgrounds.

The unity of the church is to reflect the unity of the one Lord upon which she is built. From the beginning, the multi-ethnic nature of the church went against the cultural norms. The church, as we see in Acts, wrestled with how diversity should be handled. In Acts 15, the debate was taken up with the apostles and elders. The decision was clear. The kingdom was open to Gentiles. The commitment to take the message of Jesus to all people, coupled with the power of the Holy Spirit, enabled the church to grow and reach all kinds of people.

What happened then can happen now. What message would the church send to both red states and blue states if she were able to stand as one in contrast to hard lines of political division? What example would the church be sending Generation Z and Generation Alpha if she united in worship and praise of the Lord, instead of following the cultural pattern of separation? Would they begin to see the Christian faith in a new, perhaps more relevant way? What might the church share with broken families if she were to minister with love and truth to those who are searching and struggling? If the church were united, what could she contribute to the discussion of racial harmony and justice? The most important word for the culture today is that a relationship with Jesus Christ can change everything. The church's unity matters. I have heard it said with respect to ministry, education, and many other fields of work, one has to earn the right to be heard. The church has the most important message the world needs to hear. Will we earn the right to be heard? Jesus prayed we would.

The Restoration Movement Overview

As we consider why ministering across lines of racial, cultural, and socio-economic difference matters, it is important to look at what has happened previously. I have always been a member of a Restoration Movement church. My frame of reference is the Restoration Movement, though I do know that other church groups have also wrestled with this issue. It has been a challenging issue for churches in the United States.

A Troubled Past

The Christian Churches/Churches of Christ, historically, have been reluctant to engage in discussions on the issues of peace, justice, and racial reconciliation.[259] Forty years ago, on the campuses of many Restoration Movement colleges, these issues were rarely discussed.[260] While the Restoration Movement sought to stand for what the Bible says, it often did not see that the gospel speaks to questions of justice and peace just as clearly as it addresses baptism, worship, and salvation.²⁶¹ While the Restoration Movement has added much to the theological discussion around the issues of salvation, baptism, and the assurance of salvation, it's voice has been a bit muted in the discussion of how the Bible addresses justice and diversity. Not only has there been little dialog, but there have also been structural impediments to overcome. Bible colleges and universities related to the Christian Churches/Churches of Christ did not admit black students until many years after other schools already had.²⁶² For too long, too many Christian Church/Church of Christ schools were not open to people of different backgrounds.

Richard Hughes also notes that during the time of the Civil Rights Movement, "Almost never did white, mainstream Churches of Christ support the great, swelling movement on behalf of peace and justice that captured the imaginations of so many Americans during those years."²⁶³ Hughes also provides a succinct reason for the Restoration Movement's lack of action: "While we are Christians, we are also creatures of the culture in which we live."²⁶⁴

Douglas Foster asserts that how the Restoration Movement historically dealt with issues of diversity goes back to the attitudes of the early leaders and members about slavery. Barton W. Stone endorsed the immediate abolition of slavery. James Shannon vociferously defended slavery, and Alexander Campbell held the view that slavery was wrong, but that it was not a biblical issue and should not divide the church.²⁶⁵ In the 1840's, the Methodist church and the Baptist church split over the issue of slavery. The Presbyterian church split on the eve of the Civil War in 1861. However, churches of the Restoration Movement took no position on the issue.

Positive Trends

There have been some changes, however, in Restoration Movement churches and schools. From 1998 to 2019, the number of evangelical churches that were identified as "multiracial" (those churches in which no one ethnic group comprises 80% or more of the church attenders) tripled.²⁶⁶ A growing number of multi-ethnic churches are springing up in the Restoration Movement. Bible colleges are also becoming more intentional in reaching across lines of difference to recruit students and workers. The Faith Statement of Renew.org, a Restoration Movement group of church and educational leaders, lists under "Countercultural Living," letter C which says, "We believe that Jesus invites all races and ethnicities into the Kingdom of God. Because humanity has exhibited grave racial injustices throughout history, we believe that everyone, especially disciples, must be proactive in securing justice for people of all races and that racial reconciliation must be a priority for the church."[267] These are encouraging signs for a movement that is dedicated to the desire that all people enter a relationship with the Lord Jesus Christ and restore the church to her New Testament roots.

Where Do We Go From Here?

To resolve some of these problems, Christian Church/Church of Christ schools must reframe the restoration vision. More must be seen than just the perspective of heaven and eternity. The Restoration Movement should have a message and vision for the "here and now" as well. The Restoration Movement, upon becoming committed to the importance of representing Jesus in this earthly life as well as standing for the truth of Scripture regarding eternity, can have a huge impact in this divided culture. The schools of the Restoration Movement must do all they can to become cross-centered and counter-cultural, both for this life and the eternal life to come.[268] Training cross-centered, counter-cultural leaders should be one of the objectives of Restoration Movement schools.

Final Picture

I want to end this book with what I think may be the most important reason why ministry across lines of racial, cultural, and socio-economic differences matters. I have mentioned Revelation 7:9-10 before, but I want to visit it one more time. In that passage, John writes, "After this I looked, and there before me was a great multitude that no one could count, from every nation, tribe, people, and language, standing before the throne and before the Lamb. They were wearing white robes and were holding palm branches in their hands.

And they cried out in a loud voice: 'Salvation belongs to our God, who sits on the throne, and to the Lamb.'"

The last book of the Bible presents a vision of God's kingdom in all its glory. John sees a gathering of many thousands of people. There is a sense of joy and excitement. They are wearing white robes and holding palm branches. They are there to see, to praise, and to honor one person: Jesus.

A huge crowd gathers to see, praise, and honor one dignitary. That idea made me think of a popular, but unusual Christmas movie, *The Polar Express*. Near the end of the movie, Hero Boy, Hero Girl, Know-it-All, and Billy are at the North Pole. While searching for gifts, they get separated from the other kids who are all eagerly awaiting the coming of Santa. Finally, after Billy finds his gift and confirms that he will get it, they find themselves at the front of the masses of people waiting for Santa to come. In this scene there are many children, thousands of elves, and all the residents of the North Pole gathered for Santa's appearance. Santa finally appears and the movie depicts the crowd going wild with joy, excitement, and wonder. Everyone's attention is on Santa. Hero Boy, though, can't see him. So, we hear his stressed voice, "I can't see him," against a backdrop of the thunderous applause of the masses of people. The reaction of the crowds at the North Pole seems to me to be a little like what this worship scene is like. On that day, the multitudes of people in heaven will be gathered around the throne. In my mind, I envision the crowd that John saw. The people are overcome by the excitement, joy, and wonder of being in heaven. They are in the presence of God the Father and the Lamb. In that moment, being in the presence of the Lord is their only thought. Nothing else matters.

Nothing else matters. There doesn't seem to be any concern about how much or how little melanin was in their skin while on this earth. There does not seem to be any concern about who raises their hands in worship and who doesn't. No one seems to be concerned with how they look. They are all dressed the same. No one seems to be comparing those who worship in a quiet, reflective way to those whose worship is emotional and expressive. It seems no one minds that they speak different languages. That which God used to disperse and separate people in Babel has become a non-issue in heaven. This is the picture I see. It is one of an innumerable multitude of people who are totally sold out to worshipping and praising God the Father and Jesus Christ. As I picture this scene in my head, I can almost hear the voices:

> *Erstaunliche Gnade, Was ein lieblicher Ton Einen Wicht wie mich rettete!*
>
> *Sublime gracia del Señor, que a un pecador salvó; perdido andaba, él me halló, su luz me rescató*
>
> *Katika neema ya Yesu, nimeokolewa, Nilipotea dhambini, nilikuwa kipofu rohoni*
>
> *Grâce étonnante, que le son est doux. Qui sauva un malheureux comme moi*
>
> *Graça maravilhosa! Quão doce é o som. Que salvou um miserável como eu*

The voices are in different pitches and tones. The words may start out as German, Spanish, Swahili, French, Portuguese, or English, but they seem to blend to form one beautiful message that speaks to the glory of God and the atoning work of Jesus. The song echoes in my heart and head.

> *Amazing Grace! How sweet the sound that saved a wretch like me!*

The chorus of Eliza Hewitt's hymn, written in 1898, are appropriate. "When we all get to heaven, what a day of rejoicing that will be! When we all see Jesus, we'll sing and shout the victory." On that day, we will join our neighbors in celebrating the goodness of God.

Bibliography

Alanis, Kaitlyn. "8-year-old was embarrassed after losing his hair, so his classmates lost theirs, too." *The Wichita Eagle*. February 4, 2019. kansas.com/news/nation-world/national/article225503450.html

Alexander, Michelle. *The New Jim Crow: Mass Incarceration in the Age of Colorblindness*. New York, NY: The New Press, 2020.

Alexander, T. Desmond. *From Eden to New Jerusalem*. Grand Rapids, MI: Kregel Publications, 2013.

_____. *The City of God and the Goal of Creation: An Introduction to the Biblical Theology of the City of God*. Nashville, TN: Crossway, 2018.

Allen, Scott David. *Why Social Justice is Not Biblical Justice*. Grand Rapids, MI: Credo Publishers, 2020.

Altmann, Brenton. "As a Matter of Principal-Multicultural Mission and Ministry in Lutheran Education." *Lutheran Theological Journal* 55, no. 2 (August 2021): 73-77. search.informit.org/doi/10.3316/INFORMIT.074675281239183

Aziz, Garth. "Toward A Contemporary Understanding of Youth Ministry as a Descriptive Agency." *In die Skriflig* 53, no. 1, (March 2019): 1-7. doi.org/10.4102/ids.v53i1.2403

Baeza, Ralph. *Reaching Professionals in Metropolises: Practical Strategies for the 21st Century Church*. Maitland, FL, Xulon Press, 2014.

Baker, Susan S. *Globalization, and Its Effects on Urban Ministry in the 21st Century*. Pasadena, CA: William Carey Publishing, 2009.

Bakke, Raymond J. *A Theology as Big as the City*. Downers Grove, IL: Intervarsity Press, 1997.

_____. *The Urban Christian: Effective Ministry in Today's Urban World*. Downers Grove, IL: Intervarsity Press, 1987.

Barrett, C. K. *Acts of the Apostles: A Shorter Commentary*. London, UK: Bloomsbury Publishing, 2002.

Barron, Jessica M., and Rhys H. Williams. *The Urban Church Imagined: Religion, Race and Authenticity in the City*. New York, NY: New York University Press, 2017.

Battle, Michael. *The Church Enslaved: A Spirituality for Racial Reconciliation*. Minneapolis, MN: Fortress Press, 2005.

Baucham, Voddie. "Irreconcilable Views of Reconciliation." *Grace to You,* October 18, 2019, gty.org/library/sermons-library/TM19-9/irreconcilable-views-of-reconciliation-voddie-baucham

Beale, G. K., and Mitchell Kim. *God Dwells Among Us: Expanding Eden to the Ends of the Earth.* Downers Grove, IL, Intervarsity Press, 2014.

Belew, Kathleen, and Ramon Gutierrez. *A Field Guide to White Supremacy.* Berkley, CA: University of California Press, 2021.

Blum, Edwin. *1 and 2 Peter,* Vol. 12, *The Expositor's Bible Commentary.* Edited by Frank E. Gaebelein, 209-289. Grand Rapids, MI: Zondervan Publishing Company, 1978.

Bock, Darrell L. *Acts.* Grand Rapids, MI: Baker Academic, 2007.

Boersma, Gerald P. "Fons Iustitiae: Justice in the City of God." *International Journal of Systematic Theology* 23, no. 1 (January 2021): 68-91. doi.org/10.1111/ijst.12460

Bonner, Jeanne. "Seeing a crime and not reporting it is often not a crime." CNN, July 21, 2017. cnn.com/2017/07/21/us/crime-bystanders-no-charges/index.html

Brandt, Ryan A. and John Frederick. *Spiritual Formation for the Global Church: A Multi-Denominational, Multi-Ethnic Approach.* Downers Grove, IL: Intervarsity Press, 2021.

Branson, Mark Lau, and Juan F. Martinez. *Churches, Culture and Leadership: A Practical Theology of Congregations and Ethnicities.* Downers Grove, IL: Intervarsity Press, 2023.

Bruner, Frederick Dale. *The Gospel of John: A Commentary.* Grand Rapids, MI: William B. Eerdmans Publishing, 2012.

Burge, Ryan P. *20 Myths about Religion and Politics in America.* Minneapolis, MN: Fortress Press, 2022.

Callaham, Scott, and Will Brooks. *World Mission: Theology, Strategy, and Current Issues.* Bellingham, WA: Lexham Press, 2019.

Canton, Larry. "In ministry, being there can make a difference." *Tuscaloosanews.com.* February 18, 2018. tuscaloosanews.com/story/opinion/columns/2018/02/18/port-rail-in-ministry-being-there-can-make-difference/14236891007/

Carson, D. A. *Matthew,* Vol. 8, *The Expositors Bible Commentary,* edited by Frank E. Gaebelein, 3-599. Grand Rapids, MI: Zondervan, 1978.

Carson, Penelope. "Child Labor: White Slavery." Christianity Today. History, christianitytoday.com/1997/01/child-labor-white-slavery/

Central Christian College of the Bible. *2021-2022 Academic Catalog.* Moberly, MO: CCCB, 2022.

Bibliography

Chaffrey, Tim. "Christ's Resurrection-Four Accounts, One Reality." *Answers Magazine*. April 5, 2015, answersingenesis.org/jesus/resurrection/christs-resurrection-four-accounts-one-reality/

"Child Well-Being In Single-Parent Families." Annie E. Casey Foundation. August 1, 2022. aecf.org/blog/child-well-being-in-single-parent-families#:~:text=Statistics%20About%20Children%20in%20Single,every%20three%20kids%20across%20America.

Cleveland, Christena. *Disunity in Christ: Uncovering the Hidden Forces that Keep Us Apart*. Downers Grove, IL: Intervarsity Press, 2013.

Conn, Harvie M. and Manuel Ortiz. *Urban Ministry: The Kingdom, the City, and the People of God*. Downers Grove, IL: Intervarsity Press, 2001.

Contreras, Russell. "American churches remain largely segregated — with one exception." Axios. May 18, 2023. axios.com/2023/05/18/religion-protestant-evangelical-hispanic-latino

Corbett Steve, and Brian Fikkert. *When Helping Hurts: How to Alleviate Poverty Without Hurting the Poor…and Yourself*. Chicago, IL: Moody Publishers, 2014.

"Daily Vacation Bible Schools." *Religious Education*. Vol. 2, Iss. 5, (December 1907):198. ezproxy.liberty.edu/login?

Darwin, Charles. *The Descent of Man*. London, England: John Murray, 1871.

Davis, Josh, and Nikki Lerner. *Worship Together in Your Church As in Heaven*. Nashville, TN: Abingdon Press, 2015.

De Witte, Melissa. "Conversations about race between Black and white friends feel risky but are valuable, Stanford psychologists find." *Stanford News*, September 20, 2021. news.stanford.edu/2021/09/20/conversations-race-black-white-friends-can-feel-risky-valuable/

DeYmaz, Mark. *Building A Healthy Multi-Ethnic Church: Mandates, Commitments and Practices of a Diverse Congregation*. San Francisco, CA: Jossey-Bass Publishing, 2007.

_____. *Re:MIX: Transitioning Your Church to Living Color*. Nashville, TN: Abingdon Press, 2016.

DeYmaz, Mark, and Harry Li. *Ethnic Blends: Mixing Diversity in Your Local Church*. Grand Rapids, MI: Zondervan Publishing, 2010.

_____. *Leading a Healthy Multi-Ethnic Church: Seven Common Challenges and How to Overcome Them*. Grand Rapids, MI: Zondervan, 2013.

DeYoung, Curtiss Paul. *Living Faith: How Faith Inspires Social Justice.* Minneapolis, MN: Fortress Press, 2007.

DiAngelo, Robin. "What is Race?" *Counterpoints*, 497, (2016): 98. jstor.org/stable/45157300

Doriani, Daniel M. *Matthew*, Vol. VIII, *ESV Expository Commentary.* Wheaton, IL: Crossway, 2021.

Earle, Ralph. *1 and 2 Timothy*, vol. 11, *The Expositor's Bible Commentary.* Edited by Frank E. Gaebelein, 339-418. Grand Rapids, MI: Zondervan Publishing Company, 1978.

Easley, Ernest. *Resuscitating Evangelism.* Nashville, TN: B & H Publishing Group, 2020.

Estep, James Riley. *Christian Education: A History and a Heritage.* Joplin, MO: College Press, 2024.

Everts, Don. *The Hopeful Neighborhood: What Happens When Christians Pursue the Common Good.* Downers Grove, IL: Intervarsity Press, 2020.

"Faith Statement." Renew.org. renew.org/about/faith-statement/

Fay, Bill. "Poverty in the United States." *Debt.org*, December 21, 2023, debt.org/faqs/americans-in-debt/poverty-united-states/

FBI. "History: Emmett Till." fbi.gov/history/famous-cases/emmett-till#:~:text=Milam20were%20accused%20of%20the,grisly%20details%20of%20their%20crime

Fee, Gordon D. *Revelation: A New Covenant Commentary.* Cambridge, United Kingdom: The Lutterworth Press, 2011.

Flanders, Christopher, and Werner Mischke. *Honor, Shame, and the Gospel: Reframing Our Message and Ministry.* Pasadena, CA: William Carey Publishing, 2020.

Foster, Douglas A. "Reclaiming Reconciliation: The Corruption of 'Racial Reconciliation' and How It Might Be Reclaimed for Racial Justice and Unity." *Journal of Ecumenical Studies* 55, no. 1 (Winter 2020): 63-81. doi.org/10.1353/ecu.2020.0015

_____. *The Encyclopedia of the Stone-Campbell Movement.* Grand Rapids, MI: Wm. B. Eerdmans Publishing, 2004.

Fuder, John A. *A Heart for the City: Effective Ministries to the Urban Community.* Chicago, IL: Moody Press, 2005.

Gannon, Megan. "Race is a Social Construct Scientists Argue," *Scientific American*, February 5, 2016, scientificamerican.com/article/race-is-a-social-construct-scientists

Geisler, Norman L., and William C. Roach. *Defending Inerrancy: Affirming the Accuracy of Scripture for a New Generation.* Grand Rapids, MI: Baker Books, 2012.

Bibliography

Gench, Roger J. *Theology from the Trenches: Reflections on Urban Ministry.* Louisville, KY: Westminster John Knox Press, 2014.

Gladd, Benjamin. *From Adam and Israel to the Church; A Biblical Theology of the People of God.* Downers Grove, IL: InterVarsity Press, 2019.

Goheen, Michael W. *A Light to the Nations: The Missional Church and the Biblical Story.* Grand Rapids, MI: Baker Academic, 2011.

Gordan, Wayne, and John Perkins, *Making Neighborhoods Whole: A Handbook for Christian Community Development.* Downers Grove, IL: InterVarsity Press, 2013.

Gornik, Mark L. *To Live in Peace: Biblical Faith and the Changing Inner City.* Grand Rapids, MI: William B. Eerdmans Publishing, 2002.

Gornik, Mark L., and Maria Lieu Wong. *Stay in the City: How Christian Faith is Flourishing in an Urban World.* Grand Rapids, MI: William B. Eerdmans Publishing, 2017.

Gray, Derwin L. *How To Heal Our Racial Divide.* Carol Stream, IL: Tyndale House Publishing, 2022.

Green, Michael E. *The Message of Matthew: The Kingdom of Heaven.* Downers Grove, IL: InterVarsity Press, 2020.

Gruber, Dick. *6 Children's Ministry Essentials: A Quick-Access Guide.* Edited by Dick Gruber. Springfield, MO: Gospel Publishing House, 2017.

Guilford Works. March 12, 2024. guilfordworks.org/about-us/

Hamilton, Adam. "Is the Bible Inerrant and Infallible?" *Ministry Matters.* July 15, 2021. ministrymatters.com/preach/entry/10848/is-the-bible-inerrant-and-infallible

———. *Making Sense of the Bible: Rediscovering the Power of Scripture Today.* New York, NY: Harper Collins, 2014.

———. "The Bible, Homosexuality, and the UMC—Part One." April 27, 2016.

Ham, Ken, and A. Charles Ware. *One Race One Blood: A Biblical Answer to Racism.* Green Forest, AR: New Leaf Publishing Company, 2011.

Harris, Murray J. "2 Corinthians." *The Expositor's Bible Commentary.* Grand Rapids, MI: Zondervan Publishing Company, 1976.

Harrison, Everett. F. *Romans,* Vol. 10, *The Expositors Bible Commentary.* Edited by Frank E. Gaebelein, 1-171. Grand Rapids, MI: Zondervan, 1978.

Hartke, Austen. "7 Things the Largest-Ever Survey of Transgender People Tells Us About Our Churches." December 9, 2016. sojo.net/articles/7-things-largest-ever-survey-transgender-people-tells-us-about-our-churches

Henry, Charles P. *Long Overdue: The Politics of Racial Reparations* (New York, NY: New York University Press, 2007), 20.

Hill, Wesley. *Washed and Waiting: Reflections on Christian Faithfulness and Homosexuality.* Grand Rapids, MI: Zondervan Publishing Company, 2016.

Houston, Walter J. *Justice: The Biblical Challenge.* London, UK: Routledge, 2014.

Hughes, Richard. *Reclaiming a Heritage, Updated and Expanded Edition: Reflections on the Heart, Soul, and Future of Churches of Christ.* Abilene, TX: Abilene Christian University Press, 2019.

_____. *Reviving the Ancient Faith: The Story of Churches of Christ in America.* Abilene, TX: Abilene Christian University Press, 2008.

Ince, Irwyn L. *The Beautiful Community: Unity, Diversity, and the Church at Its Best.* Downers Grove, IL: Intervarsity Press, 2020.

Iorg, Jeff. *The Case for Antioch.* Nashville, TN: B & H Publishing Group, 2011. ProQuest E-book Central.

Jablonski, Nina, and George Chaplin. *In Light of Evolution: Volume IV: The Human Condition.* Washington D.C.: National Academies Press, 2010.

Jacobs, Linda Ransom. *"The Single Parent: Confident and Successful.* Minneapolis, MN: Bethany House Publishers, 2019.

Johnson, Alan F. *Revelation*, vol. 12, *The Expositor's Bible Commentary.* Edited by Frank E. Gaebelein, 399-603. Grand Rapids, MI: Zondervan, 1978.

Kaltenbach, Caleb. *Messy Grace: How a Pastor with Gay Parents Learned to Love Others Without Sacrificing Convictions.* Colorado Springs, CO: Waterbrook, 2015.

Katongole, Emmanuel, and Chris Rice. *Reconciling All Things: A Christian Vision for Justice, Peace, and Healing.* Downers Grove, IL: Intervarsity Press, 2008.

Keener, Craig S. *Acts: An Exegetical Commentary,* vol. 1: *Introduction and 1:1-2:47.* Grand Rapids, MI: Baker Academic, 2012, ProQuest E-book Central.

Keener, Craig S. *The Gospel of John: 2 Volumes.* Grand Rapids, MI: Baker Academic, 2010.

Keller, Timothy. *Center Church: Doing Balanced Gospel-Centered Ministry in Your City.* Grand Rapids, MI, Zondervan Publishing Company, 2012.

_____. *Loving the City: Doing Balanced Gospel-Centered Ministry in Your City.* Grand Rapids, MI: Zondervan Publishing, 2012.

_____. *Generous Justice: How God's Grace Makes Us Just.* New York, NY: Penguin Books, 2010.

Bibliography

_____. "The Bible and Race," *Life in the Gospel*, Spring 2020. Accessed September 26, 2023. quarterly.gospelinlife.com/the-bible-and-race/

Key, Barclay. *Race and Restoration: Churches of Christ and the Black Freedom Struggle (Making the Modern South)*. Baton Rouge, LA: LSU Press, 2013.

Martin Luther King, Jr., "Loving Your Enemies," Dexter Avenue Baptist Church, Montgomery, AL, November 17, 1957.

Kruse, Colin. "2 Corinthians." *Tyndale New Testament Commentaries*. Grand Rapids, MI: William B. Eerdmans Publishing Company, 1987.

Kruse Colin G. *John*. Downers Grove, IL: Intervarsity Press, 2008.

LaMotte, Sandee. "Robin DiAngelo: How 'white fragility' supports racism and how whites can stop it." CNN Health, June 7, 2020. cnn.com/2020/06/07/health/white-fragility-robin-diangelo-wellness/index.html

"LGBT Rights," Gallup News, news.gallup.com/poll/1651/gay-lesbian-rights.aspx, Accessed November 3, 2022

Loyd-Paige, Michelle R., and Michelle D. Williams. *Diversity Playbook: Recommendations and Guidelines for Christian Organizations*. Abilene, TX: Abilene Christian University Press, 2021.

Longenecker, Richard. *The Acts of the Apostles*, Vol. 9, *The Expositors Bible Commentary*. Edited by Frank E. Gaebelein, 207-373. Grand Rapids, MI: Zondervan, 1978.

Loritts, Bryan. *Insider Outsider: My Journey as a Stranger in White Evangelicalism and My Hope for Us All*. Grand Rapids, MI: Zondervan, 2018.

_____. *The Offensive Church: Breaking the Cycle of Ethnic Disunity*. Downers Grove, IL: Intervarsity Press, 2023.

Lupton, Robert G. *Toxic Charity: How Churches and Charities Hurt Those They Help*. San Francisco, CA: Harper One, 2011.

Major, Barbara Crain. *Deconstructing Racism: A Path Toward Lasting Change*. Minneapolis, MN, Fortress, Press, 2023.

Martin, Ralph P., and Peter H. Davids. *Dictionary of the Later New Testament and its Developments: A Compendium of Contemporary Biblical Scholarship*. Downers Grove, IL: Intervarsity Press, 1997.

McEntire, Katie. "Unlocking Independence Safely: A Guide for Parents of Latchkey Kids." Safe Wise. September 7, 2023. safewise.com/news/unlocking-independence-safely-a-guide-for-parents-of-latchkey-kids/

McEwan, Liz. "The City Is a Mission Field (But Not Only in the Way You Think)." *The Lookout.* May 1, 2016. lookoutmag.com/2016/the-city-is-a-mission-field-but-not-only-in-the-way-you-think/

McIntosh, Gary L., and Alan McMahan. *Being the Church in a Multi-Ethnic Community: Why It Matters and How It Works.* Fishers, IN: Wesleyan Publishing House, 2012.

McNeil, Brenda Salter, and Rick Richardson. *The Heart of Racial Justice: How Soul Change Leads to Social Change.* Downers' Grove, IL, Intervarsity Press, 2022.

"Naomi Brooks et al., Appellants, v. School District of City of Moberly, Missouri, Etc. et al., Appellees, 267 F.2d 733 (8t Cir. 1959)," *Justia US Law,* Accessed October 26, 2022, law.justia.com/cases/federal/appellate-courts/F2/267/733/393864/

Newbell, Trillia J. *United: Captured by God's Vision for Diversity.* Chicago, IL: Moody Press, 2014.

Oyakawa, Michelle. "Racial Reconciliation as a Suppressive Frame in Evangelical Multiracial Churches." *Sociology of Religion* 80, no. 4 (Winter 2019): 496-517. doi.org/10.1093/socrel/srz003

Painter, John, and Scot McKnight. *Eerdmans Commentary on the Bible: Epistles of John and Jude.* Grand Rapids, MI: William B. Eerdmans Publishing, 2021.

Pappy, Annesha. "ICYMI: New Data Shows that Nearly 30% of Gen Z Adults Identify as LGBTQ+." Human Rights Campaign. January 24, 2024.

Park, Seong Hyun, Aida Spencer, and William David Spencer, eds. *A Biblical and Theological Framework for the City.* Eugene, OR: Wipf and Stock Publishers, 2013. ProQuest E-book.

Parker, Kim. "Americans' Complex Views on Gender Identity and Transgender Issues." Pew Research. June 28, 2022.

Parker, Kim, Juliana Menace Horowitz, Rich Morin, and Mark Hugo Lopez. "Chapter 5: Race and Social Connections—Friends, Family, and Neighborhoods," Pew Research Center. June 11, 2015.

Perkins, John M. *One Blood: Parting Words to the Church and Race and Love.* Chicago, IL: Moody Publishers, 2018.

Pew Research. "Chapter 6, Religion, Pew Research Center. June 13, 2013. pewresearch.org/social-trends/2013/06/13/chapter-6-religion/

Pillay, Jerry. "Racism and Xenophobia: The role of the Church in South Africa." *Verbum et Ecclesia* 38, no. 3, suppl.1 (2017): 3-17. doi.org/10.4102/ve.v38i3.1655.

Bibliography

"Poverty Status of Children by Family Structure." Office of Juvenile Justice and Delinquency Prevention. ojjdp.ojp.gov/statistical-briefing-book/population/faqs/qa01203

Prontzos, Peter G. "The Concept of Race is a Lie," *Scientific American*, Last modified May 14, 2019. Accessed September 26, 2023. blogs.scientificamerican.com/observations/the-concept-of-race-is-a-lie/

"Racially Diverse Congregations in the U.S. Have Nearly Tripled in the Past 20 Years, Baylor University Study Finds." November 11, 2020. news.web.baylor.edu/news/story/2020/racially-diverse-congregations-us-have-nearly-tripled-past-20-years-baylor#:~:text=10%25%20of%20mainline%20Protestant%20churches,multiracial%2C%20up%20from%2017%25

Rea, Hannah. "Strange Fruit: Lynching in the Midwest," *African American Midwest*, February 3, 2022.

Reader's Digest. "30 Stories about the Touching Kindness of Strangers That'll Make You Tear Up." March 9, 2024. rd.com/article/kindness-strangers/

Reardon, Sara. "Genetic Patterns Offer Clues to Evolution of Homosexuality." *Nature*. August 3, 2011.

"Released! New 2020 Statistics on Multiracial Churches." Multiethnic.church. January 8, 2020. multiethnic.church/released-new-2020-statistics-on-multiracial-churches/.

Resane, Kelebogile T. "Difficult Dialogue: A Tool Towards Racial Harmony in a Multicultural Church." *Die Skriflig* 54, no. 1 (2020): 1-8. doi.org/10.4102/ids.v54i1.2547.

Richards, Lawrence O. *Christian Education: Seeking to Become Like Jesus Christ*. Grand Rapids, MI, Zondervan Publishing Company, 1975.

Ringenberg, William C., and Mark Noll. *The Christian College: A History of Protestant Higher Education in America*. Grand Rapids, MI: Baker Academic, 2006.

"Roller Coaster Ride: Coach Williams Emphasizes Tar Heel 'Want-To.'" UNC Sports. December 6, 2013. chapelboro.com/sports/unc-sports/coach-williams-harps-tar-heel-want.

Ross, Allen P "Studies in the Book of Genesis Part 4: The Dispersion of the Nations in Genesis 11:1-9,"*Bibliotheca sacra*, 138 no 550 (1981):129. dts.edu.

Saad, Lydia. "U.S. Perceptions of White-Black Relations Sink to New Low." Gallup. September 2, 2020. news.gallup.com/poll/318851/perceptions-white-black-relations-sink-new-low.aspx.

Sailhamer, John H. *Genesis*, vol. 2, *The Expositor's Bible Commentary*. Edited by Frank E. Gaebelein. Grand Rapids, MI: Zondervan, 1978.

Sanders, Alvin, and Efrem Smith. *Uncommon Church: Community Transformation for the Common Good*. Downers Grove, IL: Intervarsity Press, 2020.

Santhanam, Laura. "A Majority of Americans Say Policing Should Be Reformed. But Most White People Still Don't Think Police Treat Black People Differently," *PBS News Hour*, May 21, 2021, pbs.org/newshour/nation/a-majority-of-americans-say-policing-should-be-reformed-but-most-white-people-still-dont-think-police-treat-black-people-differently.

Schaeffer, Francis A. *Death in the City*. Downers Grove, IL: Intervarsity Press, 1969.

Sensing, Tim. *Qualitative Research: A Multi-Methods Approach to Projects for Doctor of Ministry Theses*. Eugene, OR: Wipf and Stock, 2011.

"Sexual Attraction and Orientation." *Nemours Teens Health*. kidshealth.org/en/teens/sexual-orientation.html#:~:text=Homosexual.,Bisexual. Accessed November 3, 2022.

Shaw, Ed. *Same-Sex Attraction, and the Church: The Surprising Plausibility of the Celibate Life*. Downers Grove, IL: Intervarsity Press, 2015.

Smith, David W. *Seeking a City with Foundations: Theology for an Urban World*. Nottingham, England: Langham Partnership, 2019.

Smith, Efrem. *The Post-Black and The Post-White Church: Becoming the Beloved Community in a Multi-Ethnic World*. San Francisco, CA: Jossey-Bass, 2012.

"Sodom and Gomorrah Addresses Gang Rape, Not a Loving Relationship." The Reformation Project. reformationproject.org/case/sodom-and-gomorrah/. Accessed November 3, 2022.

Sokol, Donna Claycomb, and L. Roger Owens. *A New Day in the City: Urban Church Revival*. Nashville, TN: Abingdon Press, 2017.

Squires, John T. *Eerdmans's Commentary on the Bible: Acts*. Edited by John W. Rogerson. Grand Rapids, MI: William B. Eerdmans Publishing, 2021.

Stafford, Tim. "The Abolitionists." *Christianity Today*. History, christianitytoday.com/1992/01/abolitionists/

Bibliography

"11 stats on the religious and spiritual lives of non-binary young people." Springtide Research Institute. January 24, 2023. springtideresearch.org/post/diversity-and-gen-z/11-stats-on-the-religious-and-spiritual-lives-of-non-binary-young-people.

Steinman, Karen. *Poverty*. Folcroft, PA: National Highlights, Inc., 2016. ProQuest Ebook Central.

Structured Foundation Repair Blog. "Extreme Example of Foundation Failure." April 4, 2024, structuredfoundation.com/blog/extreme-example-of-foundation-failure/.

Tenney, Merrill C. "John," *The Expositors Bible Commentary*. Edited by Frank E. Gaebelein. Grand Rapids, MI: Zondervan Publishing Company, 1981.

"The U.S. As A New Mission Field." churchmovements.com/wp-content/uploads/sites/382/2020/11/THE-U.S.-AS-A-NEW-MISSION-FIELD-6.pdf.

Thompson, John L. *Urban Impact: Reaching the World through Effective Urban Ministry*. Eugene, OR: Wipf and Stock, 2010.

Thuận, Kiêu Công. "The Development of an Outreach Ministry to the Vietnamese Diaspora in Ulsan, South Korea: A Case Study." *Journal of Asian Mission* 21, no. 1 (2020): 35-52. Accessed September 23, 2022. go.openathens.net/redirector/liberty.edu? proquest.com/scholarly-journals/development-outreach-ministry-vietnamese-diaspora/docview/2616889623/se-2.

Towner, Philip H. *The Letters to Timothy and Titus*, Grand Rapids, MI: William B. Eerdmans Publishing Company, 2006.

Tulsa Historical Society and Museum. "1921 Tulsa Race Massacre." tulsahistory.org/exhibit/1921-tulsa-race-massacre/.

Um, Stephen T., and Justin Buzzard. *Why Cities Matter To God, The Culture and The Church*. Wheaton, IL: Crossway Books, 2013.

University of Massachusetts Amherst, April 29, 2021. umass.edu/news/article/umass-amherstwcvb-poll-finds-nearly-half.

Viviano, JoAnne. "Dignity must accompany charity, author tells Poverty Summit, The Columbus Dispatch. October 5, 2016. dispatch.com/story/lifestyle/faith/2016/10/05/dignity-must-accompany-charity-author/23330141007/.

Vogel, Schuyler. "True Easter Faithfulness." Carleton College, March 29, 2024. carleton.edu/chaplain/news/true-easter-faithfulness/.

Walker, Jeremy. *What is Repentance?* Grand Rapids, MI: Reformation Heritage Books, 2015.

Washburne, Sophie. *Racism and Racial Justice*, New York, NY: Cavendish Square Publishing, 2020.

Watson, Kevin. "Deconstructing Critical Theory: Oppressed and Oppressor." Holistic Apologetics. December 17, 2020. holisticapologetics.com/post/deconstructing-critical-theory-oppressed-and-oppressor.

Weikart, Richard. "Racism Serves Darwinism, Darwinism Serves Racism," *Evolution News and Science Today*, February 15, 2022. evolutionnews.org/2022/02/racism-serves-darwinism-darwinism-serves-racism/

Williams II, Harry Louis. *Taking It to the Streets: Lessons from a Life of Urban Ministry.* Downers Grove, IL: Intervarsity Press, 2019.

Williams Institute. "More than 5 million LGBT adults in the US are religious." UCLA School of Law, Williams Institute. October 8, 2020. williamsinstitute.law.ucla.edu/press/lgbt-religiosity-press-release/.

Wright, J. Stafford. *Ecclesiastes*, Vol. 5, *The Expositors Bible Commentary.* Grand Rapids, MI: Zondervan, 1978.

Wolff, Jonathan. "Poverty." *Philosophy Compass* 14, no. 12 (December 2019): 1-10. doi.org/10.1111/phc3.12635.

Wood, A. Skevington. "Ephesians." *The Expositor's Bible Commentary.* Grand Rapids, MI: Zondervan Publishing, 1978.

Works, Carla Swafford. *The Least of These: Paul and the Marginalized.* Grand Rapids, MI: Wm. B. Eerdmans Publishing, 2020.

Yancey, George. *Beyond Racial Division: A Unifying Alternative to Colorblindness and Antiracism.* Downers Grove, IL, Intervarsity Press, 2022

_____. George. *Beyond Racial Gridlock: Embracing Mutual Responsibility.* Downers Grove, IL: Intervarsity Press, 2006.

Endnotes

1 D.A. Carson, Matthew, vol. 8, *The Expositors Bible Commentary* (Grand Rapids, MI: Zondervan, 1984), 506.

2 Gordon D. Fee, *Revelation: A New Covenant Commentary* (Cambridge, United Kingdom: The Lutterworth Press, 2011), 85.

3 Mark DeYmaz and Harry Li, *Leading a Healthy Multi-Ethnic Church: Seven Common Challenges and How to Overcome Them* (Grand Rapids, MI: Zondervan, 2013), 20.

4 Mark DeYmaz, *Building a Healthy Multi-Ethnic Church: Mandate, Commitments, and Practices of a Diverse Congregation* (Minneapolis, MN: Fortress Press, 2020), xv.

5 William C. Ringenberg, and Mark Noll, *The Christian College: A History of Protestant Higher Education in America* (Grand Rapids, MI: Baker Academic, 2006), 29.

6 Ibid., 86.

7 Douglas A. Foster, *The Encyclopedia of the Stone-Campbell Movement* (Grand Rapids, MI: William B. Eerdmans Publishing Company, 2004), 93.

8 Timothy J. Keller, *Center Church: Doing Gospel-Centered Ministry in Your City* (Grand Rapids, MI: Zondervan Publishing House, 2012), 135.

9 Ibid., 377.

10 T. Desmond Alexander, *The City of God, and the Goal of Creation* (Wheaton, IL: Crossway Books, 2018), 23.

11 Ibid., 29.

12 Ibid., 43.

13 Ibid., 49.

14 Donna Claycomb Sokol, and L. Roger Owens, *A New Day in the City: Urban Church Revival* (Nashville, TN: Abingdon Press, 2017), 19.

15 Kiêu Công Thuân, "The Development of an Outreach Ministry to the Vietnamese Diaspora in Ulsan, South Korea: A Case Study," Journal of Asian Mission 21, no. 1, (2020), 45. go.openathens.net/redirector/liberty.edu?url= proquest.com/scholarly-journals/development-outreach-ministry-vietnamese-diaspora/docview/2616889623/se-2.

16 Alexander, *The City of God*, 23.

17 Allen P. Ross, "Studies in the Book of Genesis Part 4: The Dispersion of the Nations in Genesis 11:1-9," Bibliotheca sacra, 138 no 550 (1981):129. dts.edu.

18 Alexander, *The City of God*, 25.

19 Ibid., 23.

20 Ibid., 38.

21 T. Desmond Alexander, *From Eden to New Jerusalem* (Grand Rapids, MI: Kregel Publications, 2013), 113, ProQuest E-book Central.

22 Raymond J. Bakke, *A Theology as Big as the City* (Downers Grove, IL: Intervarsity Press, 1997), 139.

23 Ibid., 132.

24 Harry Louis Williams II, *Taking It to the Streets: Lessons from a Life of Urban Ministry* (Downers Grove, IL: Intervarsity Press, 2019), 116.

25 Susan S. Baker, *Globalization, and Its Effects on Urban Ministry in the 21st Century* (Pasadena, CA: William Carey Publishing, 2009), 146, ProQuest E-book Central.

26 Bakke, *A Theology as Big as the City*, 139.

27 Craig S. Keener, *Acts: An Exegetical Commentary*, vol. 1: Introduction and 1:1-2:47 (Grand Rapids, MI: Baker Academic, 2012), 843, ProQuest E-book Central.

28 Bakke, *A Theology as Big as the City*, 141.

29 Ibid., 142.

30 Ibid., 146.

31 Ibid., 146.

32 Jeff Iorg, *The Case for Antioch* (Nashville, TN: B & H Publishing Group, 2011), xii, ProQuest E-book Central.

33 Seong Hyun Park et al. eds., *Reaching for the New Jerusalem: A Biblical and Theological Framework for the City* (Eugene, OR: Wipf and Stock Publishers, 2013), 2, ProQuest E-book.

34 Ibid., 6.

35 Ibid., 8

36 Ibid., 16.

37 Williams II, *Taking It to the Streets*, 202.

38 Park, et al., *Reaching for the New Jerusalem*, 58.

Endnotes

39 Harvie M. Conn, and Manuel Ortiz, *Urban Ministry: The Kingdom, the City, and the People of God* (Downers Grove, IL: Intervarsity Press, 2001), 341.

40 Baker, *Globalization*, 113.

41 Ibid, 146.

42 Park, et al., *Reaching for the New Jerusalem*, 151.

43 Ibid., 160.

44 Roger J. Gench, *Theology from the Trenches: Reflections on Urban Ministry* (Louisville, KY: Presbyterian Publishing Company, 2014), 31.

45 Alexander, *The City of God*, 166.

46 Bakke, *A Theology as Big as the City*, 205.

47 Hannah Rea, "Strange Fruit: Lynching in the Midwest," African American Midwest, February 3, 2022.

48 "Naomi Brooks et al., Appellants, v. School District of City of Moberly, Missouri, Etc. et al., Appellees, 267 F.2d 733 (8t Cir. 1959)," Justia US Law, Accessed October 26, 2022, law.justia.com/cases/federal/appellate-courts/F2/267/733/393864/.

49 Kathleen Belew and Ramon Gutierrez, *A Field Guide to White Supremacy* (Berkley, CA: University of California Press, 2021), 249.

50 Laura Santhanam, "A Majority of Americans Say Policing Should Be Reformed. But Most White People Still Don't Think Police Treat Black People Differently," PBS News Hour, May 21, 2021, pbs.org/newshour/nation/a-majority-of-americans-say-policing-should-be-reformed-but-most-white-people-still-dont-think-police-treat-black-people-differently.

51 Charles P. Henry, *Long Overdue: The Politics of Racial Reparations* (New York, NY: New York University Press, 2007), 20.

52 University of Massachusetts Amherst, April 29, 2021. umass.edu/news/article/umass-amherstwcvb-poll-finds-nearly-half.

53 Robin DiAngelo, (2016). "What is Race?" Counterpoints, 497, (2016): 98, jstor.org/stable/45157300.

54 "Genetics vs. Genomics Fact Sheet," National Human Genome Research Institute, genome.gov/about-genomics/fact-sheets/

55 Megan Gannon, "Race is a Social Construct Scientists Argue," Scientific American, February 5, 2016, scientificamerican.com/article/race-is-a-social-construct-scientists-argue/#:~:text=More%20than%20100%20years%20ago,between%20different%20populations%20of%20people.

56 Charles Darwin, *The Descent of Man*, (London, England: John Murray, 1871), 48.

57 Richard Weikart, "Racism Serves Darwinism, Darwinism Serves Racism," Evolution News and Science Today, February 15, 2022, evolutionnews.org/2022/02/racism-serves-darwinism-darwinism-serves-racism/.

58 Ken Ham, and A. Charles Ware, *One Race One Blood: A Biblical Answer to Racism* (Green Forest, AR: New Leaf Publishing Company, 2011), 91.

59 John H. Sailhamer, *Genesis, vol. 2, The Expositor's Bible Commentary*, ed. Frank E. Gaebelein (Grand Rapids, MI: Zondervan, 1978), 104.

60 Timothy Keller, "The Bible and Race," Life in the Gospel, Spring 2020, quarterly.gospelinlife.com/the-bible-and-race/.

61 Bryan Loritts, *The Offensive Church: Breaking the Cycle of Ethnic Disunity* (Downers Grove, IL: Intervarsity Press, 2023), 13.

62 *Merriam Webster Dictionary*, merriam-webster.com/dictionary/racism, Accessed October 19, 2023.

63 Martin Luther King, Jr., "Loving Your Enemies," Dexter Avenue Baptist Church, Montgomery, AL, November 17, 1957.

64 Loritts, *The Offensive Church*, 58.

65 Ibid., 63.

66 Voddie Baucham, "Irreconcilable Views of Reconciliation," Grace to You, October 18, 2019, gty.org/library/sermons-library/TM19-9/irreconcilable-views-of-reconciliation-voddie-baucham

67 Williams II, *Taking It to the Streets*, 8.

68 Alvin Sanders, and Efrem Smith, *Uncommon Church: Community Transformation for the Common Good* (Downers Grove, IL: Intervarsity Press, 2020), 98.

69 Bryan Loritts, *Insider Outsider: My Journey as a Stranger in White Evangelicalism and My Hope for Us All* (Grand Rapids, MI: Zondervan, 2018), 161.

70 Williams, *Taking It to the Streets*, 10.

71 Ibid., 56.

72 A. Skevington Wood, "Ephesians," *The Expositor's Bible Commentary* (Grand Rapids, MI: Zondervan Publishing, 1978), 40.

73 Josh Davis, and Nikki Lerner, *Worship Together in Your Church As in Heaven* (Nashville, TN: Abingdon Press, 2015), 22.

74 Ibid., 23

Endnotes

75 Williams II, *Taking It to the Streets*, 63-64.

76 DeYmaz and Li, *Leading a Healthy Multi-Ethnic Church*, 68.

77 DeYmaz, *Building a Healthy Multi-Ethnic Church*, 47.

78 Loritts, *The Offensive Church*, 13.

79 Ibid., 41.

80 Kim Parker, Juliana Menace Horowitz, Rich Morin, and Mark Hugo Lopez, "Chapter 5: Race and Social Connections—Friends, Family, and Neighborhoods," Pew Research Center, June 11, 2015.

81 Melissa De Witte, "Conversations about race between Black and white friends feel risky but are valuable, Stanford psychologists find," Stanford News, September 20, 2021, news.stanford.edu/2021/09/20/conversations-race-black-white-friends-can-feel-risky-valuable/

82 Loritts, *The Offensive Church*, 37.

83 Ibid., 47.

84 Williams II, *Taking It to the Streets*, 14.

85 Ibid., 181.

86 Sokol and Owens, *A New Day in the City*, 46.

87 Ryan A Brandt, and John Frederick, *Spiritual Formation for the Global Church: A Multi-Denominational, Multi-Ethnic Approach* (Downers Grove, IL: Intervarsity Press, 2021), 23.

88 Sanders and Smith, *Uncommon Church*, 14.

89 Bill Fay, "Poverty in the United States," Debt.org, December 21, 2023, debt.org/faqs/americans-in-debt/poverty-united-states/

90 Karen Steinman, *Poverty* (Folcroft, PA: National Highlights, Inc., 2016), 18, ProQuest Ebook Central.

91 Fay, "Poverty," Debt.org, debt.org/faqs/americans-in-debt/poverty-united-states/.

92 Ibid.

93 Guilford Works, March 12, 2024, guilfordworks.org/about-us/.

94 Steve Corbett, and Brian Fikkert, *When Helping Hurts: How to Alleviate Poverty Without Hurting the Poor…and Yourself* (Chicago, IL: Moody Press, 2014), 62.

95 Ibid., 45.

96 Ibid., 32.

97 Ibid., 37.

98 Ibid., 40.

99 Ibid., 40.

100 Williams II, *Taking It to the Streets*, 9.

101 Conn and Ortiz, *Urban Ministry*, 18.

102 John Fuder, *A Heart for the City: Effective Ministry to the Urban Community* (Chicago, IL: Moody Publishers, 2005), 41.

103 Conn and Ortiz, *Urban Ministry*, 17.

104 Mark R. Gornik, and Maria Liu Wong, *Stay in the City: How Christian Faith is Flourishing in an Urban World* (Grand Rapids, MI: William B. Eerdmans Publishing Company, 2017), 39.

105 Keller, *Center Church*, 291.

106 Brenton Altmann, "As a Matter of Principal-Multicultural Mission and Ministry in Lutheran Education," Lutheran Theological Journal 55, no.2 (2021), 76, search.informit.org/doi/10.3316/INFORMIT.074675281239183

107 Murray J. Harris, "2 Corinthians," *The Expositor's Bible Commentary* (Grand Rapids, MI: Zondervan Publishing Company, 1976), 353.

108 Colin Kruse, "2 Corinthians," *Tyndale New Testament Commentaries* (Grand Rapids, MI: William B. Eerdmans Publishing Company, 1987), 122.

109 Ibid., 125.

110 Ibid, 127.

111 Brenda Salter McNeil, and Rick Richardson, *The Heart of Racial Justice: How Soul Change Leads to Social Change* (Downers' Grove, IL, Intervarsity Press, 2022), 34.

112 Loritts, *The Offensive Church*, 5.

113 McNeil and Richardson, *The Heart of Racial Justice*, 39.

114 Douglas A. Foster, "Reclaiming Reconciliation: The Corruption of 'Racial Reconciliation' and how it might be Reclaimed for Racial Justice and Unity," Journal of Ecumenical Studies 55, no. 1 (Winter, 2020), 65.

115 McNeil and Richardson, *The Heart of Racial Justice*, 48.

116 Ibid., 49.

117 George Yancey, *Beyond Racial Division: A Unifying Alternative to Colorblindness and Antiracism* (Downers Grove, IL, Intervarsity Press, 2022), 17.

118 Ibid.

Endnotes

119 Jeanne Bonner, "Seeing a crime and not reporting it is often not a crime," CNN, July 21, 2017, cnn.com/2017/07/21/us/crime-bystanders-no-charges/index.html

120 Loritts, *The Offensive Church*, 8.

121 "Roller Coaster Ride: Coach Williams Emphasizes Tar Heel 'Want-To,'" UNC Sports, December 6, 2013, chapelboro.com/sports/unc-sports/coach-williams-harps-tar-heel-want.

122 Loritts, *The Offensive Church*, 29.

123 McNeil and Richardson, *The Heart of Racial Justice*, 33.

124 Loritts, *The Offensive Church*, 47.

125 Williams II, *Taking It to the Streets*, 200.

126 *Merriam-Webster Online Dictionary*, merriam-webster.com/dictionary/sustainability?utm_campaign=sd&utm_medium=serp&utm_source=jsonld, Accessed July 25, 2024.

127 Loritts, *The Offensive Church*, 135.

128 Ibid., 139.

129 Schuyler Vogel, "True Easter Faithfulness," Carleton College, March 29, 2024, carleton.edu/chaplain/news/true-easter-faithfulness/.

130 Williams, *Taking It to the Streets*, 56.

131 Ibid., 57.

132 Gornik and Wong, *Stay in the City*, 10.

133 Ibid., 39.

134 Ibid., 85

135 Ibid., 88.

136 Sanders and Smith, *Uncommon Church*, 127.

137 Jerry Pillay, "Racism and Xenophobia: The role of the Church in South Africa," Verbum et Ecclesia 38, no. 3, suppl. 1 (2017), 11. doi.org/10.4102/ve.v38i3.1655

138 Scott Callaham, and Will Brooks. *World Mission: Theology, Strategy, and Current Issues* (Bellingham, WA: Lexham Press, 2019), 130.

139 Brandt and Frederick, *Spiritual Formation for the Global Church*, 143.

140 Sanders and Smith, *Uncommon Church*, 17.

141 Ibid.

142 Foster, *The Encyclopedia of the Stone-Campbell Movement*, 612.

143 Structured Foundation Repair Blog, "Extreme Example of Foundation Failure," April 4, 2024, structuredfoundation.com/blog/extreme-example-of-foundation-failure/

144 Norman L. Geisler, and William C. Roach, *Defending Inerrancy: Affirming the Accuracy of Scripture for a New Generation* (Grand Rapids, MI: Baker Books, 2012), 196.

145 Ibid.

146 Ralph Earle, *1 and 2 Timothy, vol. 11, The Expositor's Bible Commentary*, ed. Frank E. Gaebelein (Grand Rapids, MI: Zondervan Publishing Company, 1978), 409.

147 Ibid., 409.

148 Edwin Blum, *1 and 2 Peter, vol. 12, The Expositor's Bible Commentary*, ed. Frank E. Gaebelein, (Grand Rapids, MI: Zondervan Publishing Company, 1978,) 275.

149 Geisler, *Defending Inerrancy*, 199.

150 Adam Hamilton, "Is the Bible Inerrant and Infallible?" Ministry Matters, July 15, 2021. ministrymatters.com/preach/entry/10848/is-the-bible-inerrant-and-infallible

151 Ibid.

152 Adam Hamilton, *Making Sense of the Bible: Rediscovering the Power of Scripture Today* (New York, NY: Harper Collins, 2014), 129.

153 Hamilton, "Is the Bible Inerrant and Infallible?"

154 Tim Chaffrey, "Christ's Resurrection-Four Accounts, One Reality," Answers Magazine, April 5, 2015, answersingenesis.org/jesus/resurrection/christs-resurrection-four-accounts-one-reality/

155 Earle, *1 and 2 Timothy*, 358.

156 Philip H. Towner, *The Letters to Timothy and Titus* (Grand Rapids, MI: William B. Eerdmans Publishing Company, 2006), 156.

157 Frederick Dale Bruner, *The Gospel of John: A Commentary* (Grand Rapids, MI: William B. Eerdmans Publishing Company, 2012), 209.

158 Craig S. Keener, *The Gospel of John: 2 Volumes* (Grand Rapids, MI: Baker Academic, 2010), 569.

159 Colin G. Kruse, *John* (Downers Grove, IL: Intervarsity Press, 2008), 118.

160 Daniel M. Doriani, *Matthew, vol. VIII, ESV Expository Commentary* (Wheaton, IL: Crossway, 2021), 606.

161 Fee, *Revelation: A New Covenant Commentary*, 85.

Endnotes

162 Everett F. Harrison, *Romans, vol. 10, The Expositors Bible Commentary*, ed. Frank E. Gaebelein (Grand Rapids, MI: Zondervan, 1978), 41.

163 J. Stafford Wright, *Ecclesiastes, vol. 5, The Expositors Bible Commentary*, ed. Frank E. Gaebelein (Grand Rapids, MI: Zondervan, 1978), 1176.

164 Carson, *Matthew*, 536.

165 Darrell L. Bock, *Acts* (Grand Rapids, MI: Baker Academic, 2007), 142.

166 John Painter, and Scot McKnight, *Eerdmans Commentary on the Bible: Epistles of John and Jude* (Grand Rapids, MI: William B. Eerdmans Publishing Company, 2021), 36.

167 Harrison, *Romans*, 54.

168 C. K. Barrett, *Acts of the Apostles: A Shorter Commentary* (London, UK: Bloomsbury Publishing, 2002), 362.

169 Alan F. Johnson, *Revelation, vol. 12, The Expositor's Bible Commentary*, ed. Frank E. Gaebelein (Grand Rapids, MI: Zondervan, 1978), 484.

170 Richard Longenecker, *The Acts of the Apostles, vol. 9, The Expositors Bible Commentary*, ed. Frank E. Gaebelein (Grand Rapids, MI: Zondervan, 1978), 445.

171 John T. Squires, *Eerdmans's Commentary on the Bible: Acts*, ed. John W. Rogerson (Grand Rapids, MI: William B. Eerdmans Publishing, 2021), 64.

172 Carson, *Matthew*, 596.

173 Longenecker, *The Acts of the Apostles*, 256.

174 Ernest Easley, *Resuscitating Evangelism* (Nashville, TN: B & H Publishing Group, 2020), 7.

175 Gench, *Theology from the Trenches*, 3.

176 Conn and Ortiz, *Urban Ministry*, 64.

177 Ibid., 211.

178 Timothy Keller, *Loving the City: Doing Balanced Gospel-Centered Ministry in Your City* (Grand Rapids, MI: Zondervan Publishing, 2012), 142.

179 Williams, *Taking It to the Streets*, 8.

180 Gornik and Wong, *Stay in the City*, 10.

181 Reader's Digest, "30 Stories about the Touching Kindness of Strangers That'll Make You Tear Up," March 9, 2024, rd.com/article/kindness-strangers/.

182 Ibid.

183 Ibid.

184 Williams, *Taking It to the Streets*, 61.

185 Ibid., 56.

186 Ibid.

187 Ibid., 62.

188 Loritts, *Insider Outsider*, 28.

189 Ibid., 156.

190 Gornik and Wong, *Stay in the City*, 35.

191 Ibid., 36.

192 Larry Canton, "In ministry, being there can make a difference," Tuscaloosanews.com, February 18, 2018, tuscaloosanews.com/story/opinion/columns/2018/02/18/port-rail-in-ministry-being-there-can-make-difference/14236891007/

193 Keller, *Loving the City*, 207.

194 Williams, *Taking It to the Streets*, 200.

195 Kaitlyn Alanis, "8-year-old was embarrassed after losing his hair, so his classmates lost theirs, too," The Wichita Eagle, February 4, 2019, kansas.com/news/nation-world/national/article225503450.html.

196 Central Christian College of the Bible, 2021-2022 Academic Catalog (Moberly, MO: CCCB, 2022), 44.

197 Liz McEwan, "The City Is a Mission Field (But Not Only in the Way You Think)," The Lookout, May 1, 2016, lookoutmag.com/2016/the-city-is-a-mission-field-but-not-only-in-the-way-you-think/.

198 "The U.S. As A New Mission Field, churchmovements.com/wp-content/uploads/sites/382/2020/11/THE-U.S.-AS-A-NEW-MISSION-FIELD-6.pdf.

199 Ibid.

200 Keller, *Center Church*, 135.

201 Ibid., 143.

202 Aneesha Pappy, "ICYMI: New Data Shows that Nearly 30% of Gen Z Adults Identify as LGBTQ+," Human Rights Campaign, January 24, 2024.

203 Ibid.

Endnotes

204 Williams Institute, "More than 5 million LGBT adults in the US are religious," UCLA School of Law, Williams Institute, October 8, 2020, williamsinstitute.law.ucla.edu/press/lgbt-religiosity-press-release/.

205 Pew Research, "Chapter 6, Religion, Pew Research Center, June 13, 2013, pewresearch.org/social-trends/2013/06/13/chapter-6-religion/.

206 "Sexual Attraction and Orientation," Nemours Teens Health, kidshealth.org/en/teens/sexual-orientation.html#:~:text=Homosexual.,Bisexual. Accessed November 3, 2022.

207 "LGBT Rights," Gallup News, news.gallup.com/poll/1651/gay-lesbian-rights.aspx, Accessed November 3, 2022.

208 Kim Parker, "Americans' Complex Views on Gender Identity and Transgender Issues," Pew Research, June 28, 2022.

209 Adam Hamilton, "The Bible, Homosexuality, and the UMC—Part One," April 27, 2016.

210 "Sodom and Gomorrah Addresses Gang Rape, Not a Loving Relationship, The Reformation Project, reformationproject.org/case/sodom-and-gomorrah/, Accessed November 3, 2022.

211 Hamilton, *Making Sense of the Bible*, 158.

212 Loritts, *Insider Outsider*, 150.

213 Wesley Hill, Washed and Waiting: Reflections on Christian Faithfulness and Homosexuality (Grand Rapids, MI: Zondervan Publishing Company, 2016), 27.

214 Ibid., 24

215 Ibid., 56

216 Ibid., 23.

217 Sara Reardon, "Genetic Patterns Offer Clues to Evolution of Homosexuality," Nature, August 3, 2011.

218 "11 stats on the religious and spiritual lives of non-binary young people," Springtide Research Institute, January 24, 2023, springtideresearch.org/post/diversity-and-gen-z/11-stats-on-the-religious-and-spiritual-lives-of-non-binary-young-people.

219 Austen Hartke, "7 Things the Largest-Ever Survey of Transgender People Tells Us About Our Churches," December 9, 2016, sojo.net/articles/7-things-largest-ever-survey-transgender-people-tells-us-about-our-churches.

220 Ibid.

221 Hill, *Washed and Waiting*, 181.

Who is My Neighbor?

222 FBI, "History: Emmett Till," fbi.gov/history/famous-cases/emmett-till#:~:text=Milam%20were%20accused%20of%20the,grisly%20details%20of%20their%20crime

223 Tulsa Historical Society and Museum, "1921 Tulsa Race Massacre," tulsahistory.org/exhibit/1921-tulsa-race-massacre/.

224 Ibid.

225 Kevin Watson, "Deconstructing Critical Theory: Oppressed and Oppressor," Holistic Apologetics, December 17, 2020, holisticapologetics.com/post/deconstructing-critical-theory-oppressed-and-oppressor

226 Sandee LaMotte, "Robin DiAngelo: How 'white fragility' supports racism and how whites can stop it" CNN Health, June 7, 2020, cnn.com/2020/06/07/health/white-fragility-robin-diangelo-wellness/index.html

227 Scott David Allen, *Why Social Justice is Not Biblical Justice* (Grand Rapids, MI: Credo Publishers, 2020), 21.

228 Timothy Keller, *Generous Justice: How God's Grace Makes Us Just* (New York, NY: Penguin Books, 2010), 19.

229 Walter J. Houston, *Justice: The Biblical Challenge* (London, UK: Routledge, 2014), 6.

230 Allen, *Why Social Justice*, 23.

231 Tim Stafford, "The Abolitionists," Christianity Today, History, christianitytoday.com/1992/01/abolitionists/.

232 Penelope Carson, "Child Labor: White Slavery," Christianity Today, History, christianitytoday.com/1997/01/child-labor-white-slavery/

233 Allen, *Why Social Justice*, 43.

234 Ibid., 55.

235 Ibid.

236 Ibid., 123.

237 Ibid., 122.

238 Ibid, 127.

239 Ibid, 131.

240 Katie McEntire, "Unlocking Independence Safely: A Guide for Parents of Latchkey Kids," Safe Wise, September 7, 2023, safewise.com/news/unlocking-independence-safely-a-guide-for-parents-of-latchkey-kids/.

Endnotes

241 "Child Well-Being In Single-Parent Families," Annie E. Casey Foundation, August 1, 2022, aecf.org/blog/child-well-being-in-single-parent-families#:~:text=Statistics%20About%20Children%20in%20Single,every%20three%20kids%20across%20America

242 "Poverty Status of Children by Family Structure," Office of Juvenile Justice and Delinquency Prevention, ojjdp.ojp.gov/statistical-briefing-book/population/faqs/qa01203.

243 Lawrence O. Richards, *Christian Education: Seeking to Become Like Jesus Christ*, (Grand Rapids, MI, Zondervan Publishing Company, 1975), 41.

244 Ibid., 42.

245 Linda Ransom Jacobs, "The Single Parent: Confident and Successful, (Minneapolis, MN, Bethany House Publishers, 2019), 12.

246 Ibid., 79.

247 Ibid., 80.

248 JoAnne Viviano, "Dignity must accompany charity, author tells Poverty Summit, The Columbus Dispatch, October 5, 2016, dispatch.com/story/lifestyle/faith/2016/10/05/dignity-must-accompany-charity-author/23330141007/

249 Michael W. Goheen, *A Light to the Nations* (Grand Rapids, MI: Baker Academics, 2011), 217.

250 Dick Gruber, *6 Children's Ministry Essentials: A Quick-Access Guide*, edited by Dick Gruber, (Springfield, MO, Gospel Publishing House, 2017), 8.

251 "Daily Vacation Bible Schools," Religious Education, New Haven, CT, Vol. 2, Iss. 5, December 1, 1907, 198, ezproxy.liberty.edu/login?

252 James Riley Estep, *Christian Education: A History and a Heritage* (Joplin, MO, College Press, 2024), 351.

253 Michael E. Green, *The Message of Matthew: The Kingdom of Heaven* (Downers Grove, IL: InterVarsity Press, 2020), 334.

254 Gench, *Theology from the Trenches*, 2

255 Lydia Saad, "U.S. Perceptions of White-Black Relations Sink to New Low, Gallup, September 2, 2020, news.gallup.com/poll/318851/perceptions-white-black-relations-sink-new-low.aspx

256 Merrill C. Tenney, "John," *The Expositors Bible Commentary*, ed. Frank E. Gaebelein, (Grand Rapids, MI, Zondervan Publishing Company, 1981), 167.

257 "Released! New 2020 Statistics on Multiracial Churches," Multiethnic.church, January 8, 2020, multiethnic.church/released-new-2020-statistics-on-multiracial-churches/

258 Russell Contreras, "American churches remain largely segregated — with one exception," Axios, May 18, 2023, axios.com/2023/05/18/religion-protestant-evangelical-hispanic-latino

259 Richard Hughes, Reclaiming a Heritage, Updated and Expanded Edition: Reflections on the Heart, Soul, and Future of Churches of Christ, (Abilene, TX: Abilene Christian University Press, 2019), 51.

260 Ibid., 52.

261 Ibid., 53.

262 Ibid., 55.

263 Ibid., 53.

264 Ibid.

265 Foster, *The Encyclopedia of the Stone Campbell Movement*, 619.

266 "Racially Diverse Congregations in the U.S. Have Nearly Tripled in the Past 20 Years, Baylor University Study Finds, November 11, 2020, news.web.baylor.edu/news/story/2020/racially-diverse-congregations-us-have-nearly-tripled-past-20-years-baylor#:~:text=10%25%20of%20mainline%20Protestant%20churches,multiracial%2C%20up%20from%2017%25

267 "Faith Statement, Renew.org, renew.org/about/faith-statement/

268 Richard Hughes, *Reclaiming a Heritage*, 102.

www.ingramcontent.com/pod-product-compliance
Lightning Source LLC
Chambersburg PA
CBHW031259110426
42743CB00041B/747